FOREWORD

Here we go, book number nine and not running out of ideas yet.

I like Sussex; it's big, it's high and its breezy, it also has charming local inhabitants and probably more ghosts per acre than any other county.

It was not difficult to find sixty supposedly haunted pubs; even by word of mouth, visiting them was not quite as easy. Being a native of Royal Berkshire (you know that strip of land four miles each side of the M4) the distance to some of the more outlying Sussex pubs seemed immense. This fact and my propensity for good ale and scotch necessitated my staying the night. This in turn placed an even greater burden on my somewhat meagre resources and slim profit margin.

If one thinks of writing a book for a profit one will be sadly disappointed. If however one is realistic and looks upon it as a hobby; an enjoyable past-time that might just show sufficient returns to pay for a cheap week abroad some years hence; one will exist in hopeful limbo. Such miss quotations as *"Blessed is he who expecteth nothing,"* and *"It is sometimes better to travel hopefully than to arrive,"* spring to mind.

Come travel with me on yet another pub-crawl this time through Belloc's *"Noble and bare Downs."* Trudge to the lonely alehouses still peppering the Weald. Stagger the cobbled streets of Lewes, Brighton and Chichester. Show respect where threatening gallows once held not an inn sign but the remains of the errant footpad and seep the atmosphere from the smugglers inns, Sussex has them all.

ROGER LONG

HAUNTED INNS OF EAST SUSSEX

DEAN PLACE HOTEL	Alfriston
YE OLD SMUGGLERS INN	Alfriston
THE GATEWAY RESTAURANT	Battle
BLACKBOYS INN	Blackboys
REGENCY TAVERN	Brighton
REGENCY HOTEL	Brighton
BATTLE OF WATERLOO	Brighton
THE DRUIDS HEAD	Brighton
THE PRESTONVILLE ARMS	Brighton
THE STAG	Brighton
THE RAM AT FIRLE	Firle
KINGS HEAD	Hastings
THE STAG	Hastings
THE ROYAL STANDARD	Hastings
THE RED LION	Hooe
HANGLETON MANOR INN	Hove
THE QUEENS HEAD	Icklesham
ROBIN HOOD	Icklesham
SHELLEYS HOTEL	Lewes
THE BULL INN	Newick
HAYES ARMS HOTEL	Northiam
CROWN AND THISTLE	Northiam
HORSE AND CART INN	Peasmarsh
THE RINGMER INN	Ringmer
THE GEORGE	Robertsbridge
SEVEN STARS INN	Robertsbridge
THE KINGS ARMS	Rotherfield
MERMAID INN	Rye
THE GLOBE	Rye
UNION INN	Rye
THE WHITE VINE HOTEL	Rye
THE WISHING TREE INN	Saint Leonards
THE ROYAL VICTORIA HOTEL	Saint Leonards
NEW INN	Sidley
THE QUEENS HEAD	Winchlesea
THE ROEBUCK	Wych Cross

DEAN PLACE HOTEL
ALFRISTON

The name is obviously derived from the geographical location of the hotel.

Alfriston is justly proud of its old market cross the only one to survive in East Sussex. The village began life as a Saxon settlement straddling the River Cuckmere. It once aspired to a market town and then relaxed back into its village status.

All Alfriston's inns are ancient and architecturally pleasant. The Star, The George and The Smugglers all have individual characteristics.

The South Downs Way enters Alfriston by Star Street in the west and continues down River Lane to the riverside and bridge.

Alfriston's Saint Andrews Church is an unusual one; its stonework of square napped flints is nearly unique in Sussex. The building's marriage register dates from 1504 and is thought to be the oldest in England. Large smooth boulders strewn about the village are believed to be markers for a prehistoric cross-country ridgeway.

The Dean Place Hotel is Old England at its best and most revered. From its croquet lawn to its nine hole golf course. From its elderly ladies with their cream teas to its white shirted, collar and tied bar ladies. For just once I shall quote from the hotels advertising sheet.

"This fourteenth century creeper-covered hotel nestles chameleon-like amongst acres of landscaped gardens in the rolling Sussex countryside. The tranquillity and peace are interrupted only by the occasional appearance of the resident ghost."

Let us find out a little more about the aforementioned ghost.

Once more we have a lady, this time in an expensive blue silk dress. Late in the 19TH century, when Dean Place was a domestic residence, a maid was washing up in the back kitchen. The maid hearing a knock upon the door invited the visitor to enter. This they did, without apparently the necessity of opening the door. The maid was astounded to see a dignified lady of quality enter the room. She glided demurely across it before suddenly vanishing.

During some restoration work in the early 1900's the skeleton of a woman was found under the floor. It is assumed that this was the earthly remains of our lady in blue silk. It is also assumed that she died violently, had she not there would have been little point in concealing the body.

Unfortunately there are few family records appertaining to Dean Place and at the turn of the century forensic science could not establish the age of the remains.

Over the years there have been regular sightings of the lady in blue. A five year old girl, a guest at the hotel, reported seeing the spectre in the sixties. There have been various other reports, some as recent as the mid-nineties.

A nice intriguing little mystery this, we shall never know whom this beautiful lady was or what atrocity befell her.

YE OLD SMUGGLERS INN
ALFRISTON

This particular board is seen all over the country and celebrates the illicit carrying of contraband. These boards are generally seen on the coast but a few, as this one, are found slightly further inland.

This particular inn was for a long time named after Alfristons famous market cross. The Market Cross Inn had always been nicknamed 'The Smugglers' because of the nefarious activities associated with it. Finally it took on the name officially.

This Inn was for many years the base of the Alfriston gang led by Stanton Collins. The gang used the river and complicated local paths for their illicit trafficking. Collins once led an excise man to his death on some nearby cliffs. He was later arrested for sheep stealing and transported.

The Smugglers was an ideal situation for men like Collins. A story is told that no less than eight of his men climbed into its massive chimney when the place was raided. It is also stated that the Inn had only three double bedrooms but contained 47 doors. If ever a house seemed purpose built for smuggling it is this particular construction.

Internally very little appears to have been altered in the Smuggler's Inn. There is a vast inglenook with a bread oven implanted and above the 'nook' every conceivable domestic and agricultural implement has been arrayed. The usages of the majority are obscure even to an ageing country boy such as myself. There are of course the inevitable horse brasses and the main beam has been adorned by dry hops. There is also an unusual collection of race tickets above the bar. As far as the ghost is concerned I could find no one who had any first hand knowledge. There were however locals who had heard stories and I was told of strange appearances as recently as the nineties but could not find the source. Obviously any phenomena are attributed to Stanton Collins and Co.

It was once said that if God did not exist it would be necessary to invent him. On the same theme, this old inn lends itself to be haunted. The setting is perfect, it would be easy to invent a spirit here.

In desperation I chatted to the landlord and brought the subject subtlety around to ghosts.

"I have heard the stories," he stated "But have yet to experience anything. I find the old place has the most benign of atmosphere's."

I whole-heartedly concur but whoever decided a spirit should be of a recalcitrant nature?

Some ghosts are the most amiable and friendly *people* I have ever met.

Whilst in Alfriston would be ghost hunters should seek out a Georgian house named Tuckuar. It is reputed to have a plethora of ghosts including an old man in a leather apron, an old lady who tucks people into bed and a spectral cat. The priest's house in the village is also haunted. On the Seaford Road is an area named White Way, it was here in the 18TH century that a young man and his dog were murdered by cut-throats. Their spirits are reputed to appear every seven years.

THE GATEWAY RESTAURANT
BATTLE

A very adroit and intelligent guess as to how The Gateway Restaurant obtained its name could be a little to do with its geographical location. It resides in the shadow of the mighty gatehouse of Battle Abbey.

Battle is as we all know the true site of the so called Battle of Hastings in 1066 and all that. To pinpoint the site with accuracy it was just to the south-west of the Abbey gate. Obviously the Abbey did not exist until after the Battle. William of Normandy vowed that should the day be his he would build an Abbey in commemoration of the event. As we know the day was William's, he affected to flee with a small force creating an ambush as Harold's English carelessly pursued him. Harold of course died in the Battle and William out of respect erected the high altar at the exact spot where he fell.

William constructed Saint Martin's Abbey shortly after the Battle. It was consecrated in 1094 but later became a victim of Henry VIII's reforms. Part of the Abbey that was not destroyed became a girl's school. The nearby Church of Saint Mary and the Deanery (1669) may also be visited. The George Inn is worth a call and a plaque on what once was 'The Green' informs us of bullbaiting activity.

I have made a rule in this book that only haunted pubs, inns and hotels are to be included. Rules are for the obedience of fools and the guidance of wise men. Ergo the inclusion of The Gateway Restaurant at Battle. Having heard about the haunting by a very roundabout route I dropped into the restaurant one Saturday morning in July. The middle aged and very well-dressed entrepreneur was just going out, leaving other customers and myself in the hands of his waitresses. They seemed to be mass-produced; each one blond, attractive, efficient and dressed in a white blouse and micro length black skirt. This man is to be applauded in his choice of décor, vitals, wine and staff. The latter were very busy so it seemed inappropriate to enquire about the Gateway's spiritual feline.

There is very little to say about the Gateway's spectral cat. Nothing has been recorded and the little I know is hearsay. The cat is black, presumably of male gender and has been witnessed by several customers gliding along a corridor before disappearing through a wall. There you have it.

Those who find the story of the disappearing cat rather small beer might find a little more variation of spirits around the ruined Abbey gatehouse. Naturally Harold haunts the nearby ridge where he met his fate. There is also the essential moaning monk, probably bewailing the dissolution of Battle Abbey in 1538. A spectral knight in armour, who might well, be one of Harolds stalwarts. This gentleman, complete with a large sword, was spotted by a young boy visiting the Abbey in 1971. There is also the shade of a lady who is thought to be the Duchess of Cleveland who rented the Abbey for sometime.

BLACKBOYS INN
BLACKBOYS, EAST SUSSEX

Black boys were once quite popular as inn signs and generally represented the coloured servants that the better off employed. The inference of this was that the inn had sufficient servants to look after ones welfare. The name blackamoor received some popularity at the turn of the century. A blackamoor being a native of Morocco or Bermuda, whereas a black boy was generally from the plantations. Having now described black boys in general I must admit that this particular inn was obviously called after the village in East Sussex with this unique name.

The village of Blackboys stands just east of Uckfield on the A265; a short distance to the south-east of the village stands Old Possingworth Manor. It was built in 1657 by Thomas Offley, once Lord Mayor of London. The Blackboys Inn is the epitome of English pubs. Its comfortable interior and striking exterior make it a welcome oasis on what was once a very lonesome road. Apparently the inn was built as a farmhouse in 1389. If so, it has been much altered and I noticed there is a circa 1790 sign above the door. I sat by the duck pond and engaged in conversation with some locals. I brought the conversation around to the resident ghost. I knew that Andrew Green, our most prestigious of phantom hunters, had done a report on the building. The locals seemed to concur with his observations. As far as I can ascertain there has been very little evidence other than a noisy set of phantom footsteps and a pronounced drop in temperature. For reasons that seem a little tenuous to say the least this phenomenon has been attributed to one Anne Starr. Anne was a landlord's daughter in the 18TH century. She became firstly impregnated and then abandoned by the equivalent of a travelling salesman. Reports vary greatly as to whether she lost the child, died in childbirth or committed suicide before or after the event. It is also possible that she or they lived happily ever after.
So there you have it, anything vaguely connected with the supernatural at the Blackboys Inn is attributed to our Annie.

REGENCY TAVERN
BRIGHTON

The sign once again is celebrating the Regency period and its design of architecture.

Brighton, I shall not be arrogant or foolish enough to try and describe Brighton in a couple of paragraphs. This romantic of old towns has oft been described before by observers more eloquent then I. I shall therefore just mention a 'few places to see'.

1. Architecturally The Grand and The Metropole hotels are worth seeing
2. Universities
3. Art college
4. Theatre
5. Racecourse
6. The unique Pavilion
7. The world famous Lanes
8. The Palace Pier
9. The Booth Museum of Natural History
10. The Aquarium
11. The marina and Volk's electric railway
12. Preston Manor, who's furniture hasn't changed since World War I

The Regency Tavern is as flamboyant and extrovert as the good Prince Regent himself. It is a characterful pub full of characters. One cannot generalise upon its clientele, theatrical performers and company directors rub shoulders with building labourers and jolly jack tars. There are as many professions as there are social classes and as many different hobbies as there are sexual persuasions blended in the compound of good cheer, that is the Regency Tavern.

There seems to be always something going on here. The pub has a large interior undermined and belied by its small frontage. I revisited this pub on a March Sunday lunchtime and it was, as always, bursting at the seams. I took a stool beneath a host of cherub like figurines and under some wonderfully colourful flower depicting wooden shields. The shields or plaques have a colour intensity akin to barge pictures, they are worth a visit just to observe.

I did not question the busy staff on its supernatural visitations. I knew the stories well and had regularly discussed them with locals. The Regency Tavern enjoys visitations from two separate spirits. There have been stories that one or the other or both have been laid by a medium. I doubt this is the case as both have been witnessed quite recently.

Ghost one is a little crippled girl who lived on the premises about 100 years ago. At the time The Regency Tavern was a cobblers shop and the little girl was the owners daughter. Gas lighting was in its infancy as far as domestic use was concerned. The cobbler had had gas installed and had forewarned his family of its dangerous properties. Stories vary a little but a consensus of opinion states that the little girl had been locked in her bedroom for some small misdemeanour. Thinking or convincing herself she smelt gas she launched herself through the window and died on the cobbles below. The little cripple's shade has been witnessed on many occasions over the years. It was thought that a pair of her specially made clogs found in the cellar after her death attracted her earth bound spirit. I can give no information as to the final resting-place of the shoes, but if destroyed, they have encouraged rather than discouraged this tiny spirit.

Ghost two is a tall and slender grey haired lady who kept the tavern for decades. A peaceful and resilient lady is this who has been witnessed passing through walls. It is thought that being the licensee was her whole life and now she finds it impossible to leave the building after death.

REGENCY HOTEL
BRIGHTON

For an explanation of this board please refer to Brighton's Regency Tavern. Also apparently please refer to the Regency Tavern for the story I shall try to explain.

This private hotel is well-placed amongst a thousand such other buildings in Brighton. It is about a stones throw from the aforementioned Regency Tavern and this is not the only similarity.
I had no idea of the Regency Hotel's existence or of it's haunting until I read Andrew Green's excellent book on modern Sussex hauntings. I was more than a little surprised to see Mr Green attribute the well-known supernatural happenings at the Regency Tavern to the Regency Hotel. I refer of course to the events I have described previously, the little cripple girl who leapt to her death after suspecting a gas leak.
I am perplexed. I have heard this story attributed to the Regency Tavern from a dozen different sources and I expect it to be the correct venue. However, nobody can speak with 100% authority on this subject, obviously there is no acid test so I shall attempt to look further into this case.

BATTLE OF WATERLOO
BRIGHTON

Of the many boards commemorating famous battles or campaigns e.g. Alma, Sebastopol, Trafalgar, Inkerman etc. etc. The Waterloo is probably the most common. It is a little unusual though to see it preceded by the word Battle.

As mentioned above this inn probably dates from the time of Waterloo. It is a romantic pub, this in spite and not because of its surroundings. Rock Place is a narrow street, it is one-way down to the coast, parking, forget it. It is a good pub to stroll to on early summer's evening or to drop in to on Sunday lunchtime.

I generally sit outside the Battle, weather permitting, but the interior is worth seeing. It is a long slim bar room with pictures of gentlemen dressed in the uniforms associated with the famous battle adorning the walls. There is also a newspaper clipping entitled 'The little man at Waterloo', it is a worthwhile story but too long to go into in detail here.

Have you ever wondered if ghosts are plagued with the same inconveniences of mortal men? I ask this question because the ghost at the Battle of Waterloo is most often witnessed in the 'gents'. A spectral man thought to be a coachman by his attire has been sighted by various employees over a number of years. Other than the one episode in 1996 when a decorator saw him entering the front door the spectre seems dedicated to the gents lavatory. Have you ever had the impression that you are being watched whilst performing this most necessary of functions and on turning found nobody to be there? Thought provoking isn't it.

Back to the ghost. The story goes that in the 19TH century the Mayor of Brighton and his daughter were being driven to some worthy function. A highwayman appeared, shot and killed both men and made off with the mayor's daughter. Legend dictates that the two were never heard of again and infers that the young lady was in on the act.

Where this unusual event took place we are not informed. It does not sit comfortably with me. Newspapers were tolerably well-advanced in the 19TH century and the murder of a mayor would be well-reported. It would also be a notoriously inconvenient place for an ambush.

Here is a most unlikely and flippant scenario. Could it be that the coachman was not slain but fled into the inn. His state of terror may have left him no choice for his supposedly haunted venue.

THE DRUIDS HEAD
MARKET STREET, BRIGHTON

As commonly known the Druids were an ancient order of Celtic priests. It is somewhat unusual for one to be celebrated on an inn sign. It is always possible that the location pre-dated the hostelry i.e. a place that has long been associated with Druids later becomes a built up area. An inn is then often named after the situation.

There is some conjecture as to the age of The Druid's Head. There is a large flat stone in the bar that definitely states 1510 but I am reliably informed that the building was not granted a licence until 1830 or 1855. It is described as an ex-fisherman's and smugglers inn. However, as the majority of the former indulged in the practises of the latter there was very little difference in the trades.

With reference to the smuggling trade it is pointed out that there are two sealed tunnels in the cellar, one leading to the beach and the other to the Royal Pavilion. It will be noted elsewhere in this book and others, that personally I am not a great believer in the existence of subterranean passages.

A third profession to use The Druid's Head was the London carriers. Massive delivery carts were once squeezed between the walls of the adjoining narrow lanes. The loading and unloading of the same was an asset to local employment.

Today The Druid's Head has changed little. It is still a double fronted construction of napped local sea flints. The genuine flagstone floor still exists as do the ancient ship timbered beams. The Druid's Head is now part of a vast group but seemingly this has not as yet been detrimental to its unique atmosphere. Obviously it is pursuing dining in a slight preference to wining. When I dropped in one Sunday lunchtime the staff seemed a little surprised that I had only called for a drink. There are possibly two ghosts at The Druid's Head, a cowled figure who has been witnessed under the stairway in the main bar and a lady in red who moved swiftly towards the same stairway before vanishing. That is about the sum total of inexplicable and supernatural incidents at The Druid's Head.

THE PRESTONVILLE ARMS
BRIGHTON

The sign is related to the area near which the pub stands. Preston Manor is but a short journey.

Yours truly however did not know this and was informed that The Prestonville was down near The Lanes. After a fruitless search on foot of that area I was finally directed to the inn some two miles away. The Prestonville (known locally as the Pentonville) is well-worth a visit. It has a large horseshoe shaped bar and a wooden floor. I find both of these features attractive in any licensed establishment. The walls are of great interest. There are displays of memorabilia without that overdone and cluttered effect that so often accompanies such presentations. Here we have collections of cigarette cards including those richly coloured silk flags that are almost impossible to obtain. There are sepia photographs of old Brighton and preserved national newspaper front pages announcing such earth shattering statements as 'Hitler is Dead'. I sat under a large turn of the century advertisement for a fat female trombone player and browsed through a copy of the Prestonville Post. I has already chatted to the barmaid and subtly brought the subject around to the supposed haunting. She denied all knowledge so I must rely on what is generally known.

In the 1960's the Prestonville Arms was inflicted by a type of harmless poltergeist activity. It did not last long and was restricted to the movement of heavy crates and bottles in the cellar. One wonders that if the landlord had been able to train such a spirit he might have been able to cut down on his staff.

There is little more to be said. The activity ceased as abruptly as it had started. I doubt very much if there is anything supernatural at present but the pub is still worth a visit for its ambience alone.

THE STAG
UPPER BEDFORD STREET, KEMPTOWN, BRIGHTON

For an explanation of The Stag board please refer to the Hastings entry.

A nice versatile pub is The Stag; it seems to cater for most tastes. It is some 300 years old, far outdating most of the surrounding buildings. Inside nothing is unique but everything is pleasant and efficient. There are the inevitable horse brasses, some attractive photographs of old Brighton and a nosy overfed cat.

There has been some mild poltergeist activity here but even that has deteriorated over the years. The management and staff seem a little disappointed over this. The poltergeist was quite harmless and his activities were playful rather than spiteful. 'Albert' as he is nicknamed remained popular with customers and staff alike. Albert's favourite little trick was to regularly disconnect the gas lines to the beer kegs. He also plays havoc with light switches and opens and shuts doors. One of Albert's more strenuous accomplishments was to roll a barrel down the cellar stairs.

It has been suggested that the impish joker was once a landlord at The Stag. As far as I can ascertain this assumption is based on the one sighting of the spirit. Albert is described as a tall man dressed in a large apron and wearing black armbands. Other evidence supporting the ex-landlord theory is that most of the mischief it targeted towards the more modern elements of the pub. For instance, good old real ale is never tampered with, only your modern gas filled frothless liquid inflames Albert's spectral wrath. I have every empathy with him. Incidentally after some years of placitude Albert seems to be making a comeback.

The keen and very patient ghost hunter in Brighton could spend a week looking for various reported spectral beings. A black hooded figure that strolls between gravestones in a churchyard near The Lanes. Or seeking out a badly mutilated woman with bloated limbs. This less than attractive murder victim terrorises the inhabitants of Upper Rock Place. There is also the plate-smashing poltergeist at a restaurant in Ditchling Road, or Lady Edona whose lover drowned at Worthing Point. She has walked Brighton awaiting his return since the

15

14TH century. Occasionally at midnight on May 17TH the spectral ship that she waits is seen briefly off the coast.

Back to The Lanes for a quick glimpse of a phantom who once scribbled messages on a shop ceiling. Mediums in Kemptown once provoked a troupe of dead actors who proceeded to knock on windows in the area.

Preston Manor has a spectral lady in white and a grey lady was seen in the Theatre Royal in 1960, this same venue also has a phantom nudger. The Royal Pavilion is haunted in turn by the Prince Regent, a lady thought to be Maria Fitzherbert and some ghostly footsteps presumed to come from a tunnel thought to connect with the Druid's Head.

A pre-reformation nun has been seen and heard in The Lanes. Martha Gunn a favourite dipper (person who assisted bathers) of the Prince Regent haunts the kitchens of the Royal Pavilion. In a stationer's in East Street a headless monk materialises and blood seeps through the wall on an unremarkable house on Brighton's northern borders.

Good hunting.

THE RAM AT FIRLE
FIRLE

The Ram is not as common a sign as might be supposed. One would not imagine this to be the case especially in rural settings. There are rare signs showing the ram as an implement of warfare. I believe also that I have come across 'The Battering Ram' on one occasion. Exceptions proving the rule the vast majority of ram inns are in appreciation of the Worshipful Company of Cloth Weavers. Famous individual rams are sometimes celebrated on boards. If a particular ram has been extremely powerfully built or a sexual athlete it is possible that it be remembered on a local inn sign.

Firle originated from cottage buildings belonging to a stately home. Firle Place is a splendid (mostly) Georgian building. The older part of the house is reputed to have originated in the 1400's. The building contains some excellent English furniture and a collection of old masters. It has been home to the Gage family for hundreds of years; the family's brasses and monuments may be seen in the local church. Several miles to the south stands the impressive Firle Beacon (713 feet).

The village has changed little over the centuries. There is a church, a museum, a store (circa 1780) and numerous creeper covered cottages. The Ram was obviously intended as a local pub but stood little chance of remaining so in such a picturesque hamlet. Inside we have several rooms each with an open fire and converging on a central bar. A large room at the rear of the building announces itself as 'The Courtroom'. I do not know if the room ever performed such a function but verderer's courts (responsible for law and order in the royal forests) were commonplace in old inns. Pictures of the village and assumed villagers at the Lewes bonfire celebrations adorn the walls. There are also cards advertising homespun cottage industries in the area, a local violinmaker must be almost unique. This is most definitely hiking country as several tracks traverse the village and a goodly proportion of the inn's trade comes from such groups. Indeed, as I left some 30 walkers were removing their boots at the door.

Finally to The Ram's ghost.

In late Victorian times a young local woman scraped a living as a basket maker. She suffered from a badly deformed leg that caused her to walk with a pronounced limp. The landlord took pity on the woman and permitted her to use his attic as her workshop. The unhappy woman was found dead there one morning. Always frail and vulnerable it must be assumed that she died of natural causes. The ill-fated basket maker has been held responsible for the many unnatural sounds that have been detected over the years. The noises have been likened to those of a person depending heavily upon a crutch or stick. I am led to believe that such sounds have been heard quite recently by a number of villagers. As far as I can ascertain there has never been a visual confrontation.

There we have it, before leaving however one cannot but reflect whimsically on the wisdom and practicality of offering a badly crippled woman the highest room in the building.

Avid ghost hunters in the village should return to Firle Place before journeying on. Here we have yet another spectral lady in grey. She is thought to be Margaret Kemble, the wife of General Sir Thomas Gage, Commander-in-Chief of the British forces during the American War of Independence.

KINGS HEAD
HASTINGS

This sign is an ingratiation with royalty. It may commemorate any one of a dozen monarchs the favourites being Henry VIII closely followed by Charles I, William IV and the many Georges, who are usually specifically named. A good outsider, possibly unique, is Henry VI who is depicted on the sign of the Kings Head at Islington.

Hastings is a pleasant and invigorating Sussex town. It offers the present day amusements of a seaside town whilst remaining faithful to it's traditional past. The one date and happening that all schoolchildren remember is '1066, The Battle of Hastings'. This is however geographically incorrect. The Battle of Hastings actually took place six miles to the north-west in the aptly named village of Battle.

Forgetting the Battle, Hastings has plenty of history of it's own. It has its ruined castle built by William the Conqueror. There is sufficient of this still remaining to warrant a visit. Nearby and well-worth a visit are Saint Clement's Caves, once used by the town's resident smugglers they are now one of the towns showpieces. The Town Hall displays a 243 feet long tapestry that was woven by embroiders to celebrate the 900 years since the Conquest.

There is a fishermen's museum and some almost unique wooden fishermen's huts, known locally as 'shops'. First used in the 16TH century these three storey structures were specifically designed for the drying of nets.

The extremely picturesque and narrow streeted old town is worth a visit; not the least of reasons being it is inundated with ancient pubs.

The King's Head stands on the corner of Courthouse Street and what is now the wider and busier expanse of The Bourne. I have known the old pub for sometime but was unaware of its haunting reputation until recently. A local's pub is the King's Head, just a few too many yards from the front to be plagued by the ice cream and kiss-me-quick brigade. Its largish bar with walls adorned by delicate pictures of Edwardian ladies in elegant gowns seems far removed from the grisly story that initiated the haunting.

To be honest I first read of this less than pleasant episode in an account by Andrew Green, since however I have had it verified from several sources.

In the 1770's the staff of the inn lived on the premises. One, a scullery maid, was often found wanting in her duties and was beaten by the master. On one particular evening, the innkeeper became a little over zealous in his chastisement of the maid, to such a degree in fact, that after the beating the poor girl just managed to creep to her bed. There she died of her wounds. I am told that the event is quite well-documented but I should be inclined to doubt this. In the 1770's one could do what one liked with one's staff short of actually slaying them. Such an event would cause much publicity and the perpetrator would definitely be brought to justice. Be that as it may the young scullery maid haunts the King's Head. She has been witnessed on numerous occasions. Unfortunately the bedroom which the small shade haunted was later reconstructed as a toilet. I am told that once again an intense feeling of being watched whilst at the most private of personal indulgences often prevails.

THE STAG
ALL SAINTS STREET, HASTINGS

The stag is a sign that was popular with huntsmen. Hunts often met at inns displaying the sign. On many boards stags are coupled with various other members of the animal kingdom e.g. Stag and Hounds, Stag and Pheasants. About the country there are also 'Stags Heads', 'White Stags' and in one case 'The Three Stags Heads'. A not unusual sign is 'The Baldfaced Stag'. These inns generally owe their signs to a particular animal killed in the area. Baldfaced stags have a white stripe running from their forehead to their nose. Years ago such an animal would be decapitated and the original head stuffed and used as an inn sign.

The Stag inn stands on a rampart type pathway some feet above All Saints Street. Structures like this are fairly normal in Hastings old town. The Stag is ancient and looks it. The bar is dual levelled and attractive, it has however one less than attractive feature. Opposite a picture of the regal 'Monarch of the Glen' is a glass case fixed to the wall not for any security reasons one would think. The case contains the dehydrated remains of a couple of cats and what appears to be a couple of rats. Over the years I have often pondered upon these unbecoming relics and wondered how they originated. I am told that they were discovered when building work was being done to the interior. It was not unknown in Tudor times to place cats in wall cavities to bring good luck. I have heard this story about many old buildings but I have never been able to ascertain as to whether the unfortunate feline was placed in his final abode alive or dead. Either way it could not have been the cat's lucky day.

Incidentally I have a friend who extended her ancient property in Glastonbury only to find the skeleton of a baby between the walls. Apparently unchristened offspring that died at birth could not be buried in consecrated ground. But I digress. The spirit at the Stag Inn would seem to be that of a highwayman of the Turpin era and he has been witnessed on several occasions. One unimpressed observer supposed the apparition to be part of a local pageant that was going on at the time.

I am pleased that the locals have decided that this is not a personal appearance of Dick Turpin. This vastly romanticised highwayman is the most overworked spirit in the country. I once had a lady phone me from Twyford in Berkshire to inform me that her abode was haunted by Dick Turpin.

"How do you know its Turpin?" I asked.

She went on to describe a manner of dress including doeskin breeches, pistol butts and French cocked hats (Alfred Noyes has a lot to answer for).

I respectfully pointed out that nearly four million men dressed in such a way at one time and that her supernatural intruder might be any one of them. She would not be swayed.

To return to the Stag Inn and its tolerably frequent spectral visitor. Could it not be Dick Whittington keeping an eye on his faithful companion!

Whatever did happen to Dick's cat?

It can't still be living happily ever after. Not this side of the veil anyway.

THE ROYAL STANDARD
HASTINGS

The sign of The Royal Standard is yet another patriotic sign. It is pretty general in all parts of the country but the Hastings pub has a specific reason for being so called. Folklore dictates that it was named after King Harold's standard that was placed at nearby Senlac during the Norman invasion, 1066 and all that.

I called into The Royal Standard one May evening after perusing the old town. I had inspected a dozen or more second hand book shops and at least as many pubs.

The Royal Standard is not an old pub, probably 130-150 years of age. It is well-kept, functional and boasts an aviary and children's play area. The interior is awash with naval paraphernalia, there would seem to be a plethora of accoutrements, apparatus and appurtenances connected with the senior service. However, it is all very skilfully contrived so as not to appear overcrowded. As one might suspect the landlord is an old sea dog. The staff have placed a warning notice to customers which states 'Do not engage the landlord with talk of the navy, you will be bored to death.'

I took the advice and engaged the landlord in various other themes of conversation.

"What are you doing here?" he asked. The inference being that I was too scruffy to be a grockle and not intelligent looking enough to be a twitcher.

Fortified by the vast quantity of scotch and bitter I had consumed and thus void of all inhibitions I admitted to being a writer of ghost stories. I went on to point out that I had come to the old town to have a look at The Kings Head and The Stag amongst others.

"Have you one here?" I asked, expecting a negative answer.

"Funny you should ask that," he answered "sometimes when I am tidying up on my own late at night I hear the toilet seat crash down. There is never anybody about, and, as you can imagine, it is a bit unnerving."

The landlord went on to explain that he had checked the simple mechanics of the seat, the angle of leaning and the possibility of a practical joke, but nothing could explain this phenomenon.

"Perhaps it's the roll of the ship," I suggested.

His light chuckle seemed to verge on sympathy.

Hastings has rich pickings for the enthusiastic and very patient spook hunter. The castle alone has a host of spectral people and objects. Thomas à Becket, he was dean here for sometime, is the most famous spectre. Less famous spirits are the inevitable ghostly nun and a phantom woman carrying a child. There is also ghostly music and the rattling of chains. Most spectacular of all, albeit slightly suspect, is the appearance out at sea of the castle itself. I jest not; it has been a well-witnessed spectre over the years. The castle appears in all its previous glory, not in its present state, but like an enticing Camelot, some miles away from the coast. Make of that what you will.

There are supposedly church bells buried under the sands at Bulverhythe, which ring in stormy weather. There is reportedly a young lady hitch-hiker who boards your car on the A21 and alights near Claremont School. Saint Helens Hospital, now defunct, has heavy footsteps that upset a local radio station that was broadcasting from there. In the Bohemian area a house boasts of a man in gaiters and also a group of spectral children. Andrew Green informs us that the Millers house on Windmill Hill has a spiritual lady in a paisley top and the White Rock Theatre boasts an elderly male in a dirty raincoat who disappears on sight. Don't you notice that elderly men in dirty raincoats have a habit of doing that?

Back to the female of the species, there is a spectral lady in blue reported from Guestlings Broomham School and a lady dressed in black who walks the streets of the old town. There is a second lady in black who appears at the bedside at a guesthouse very close by. Could this be one and the same I wonder. If so, it must be later in life as one is described as young and slim and the other elderly and rotund.

Do spirits age like us mortals? There's a thought.

THE RED LION
HOOE, Near BATTLE, EAST SUSSEX

The Red Lion is one of the top five most popular boards in the country. It owes its popularity to John of Gaunt but there are connections with various other royal personages.

Hooe has been sprinkled rather than sewn into rural Sussex. One notices a church spire here and an inn there with a manor house around the corner. The centre of the village, if centre there be, seems to congregate in the vicinity of The Red Lion. Here at least is a store, a phone box and several rural entrepreneurs displaying second hand cars from semi-residential premises. The street in which The Red Lion stands is charming and friendly; you might expect your dear old gran to emerge from any doorway.

Opinions vary as to the date of the origin of The Red Lion. I was informed by one source that it was built in 1595 and from another that it had been licensed since 1495. What is not in doubt is that the old building was once a smugglers paradise. The surrounding ground was formerly a tidal marsh where contraband was easily unloaded. The massive fireplace is reputed to have been a safe hiding place for French brandy and a once totally illegal tobacco mill is said to have been in existence in the attic. Tobacco came from France in sheets or blocks and needed to be ground prior to use. There is a list of ex-landlords displayed at The Red Lion and closeby an account of an affray, in 1751, between smugglers and customs men. Apparently the officers were put to rout and retreated back to Hastings.

There may be several ghosts at The Red Lion but the one most regularly witnessed is a large man in a great coat. He was most probably a seaman or an ex-landlord or both. He was in no doubt a smuggler, nearly all seaside residents were. However, this gentleman appeared to two ladies one day and they seemed convinced he was a farmer. There is still a third case that he may be a blacksmith who kept the adjacent smithy until the 1880's. Andrew Green is firmly of the opinion that the spectre is an ex-landlord by the name of James Blackman. Blackman was a member of the Groombridge gang that shifted smuggled goods up country to the Ashdown Forest villages. Mr Green also informs us that the lime trees that grew outside were a smugglers sign that this was a freehouse safe from customs officers.

Whoever the large man is or was he might or might not be the cause of the rambling footsteps upstairs and the perpetrator of the ghostly turning of the illicit tobacco mill. Of the former I would think probably so, the latter I find more doubtful, this was women's work.

This fine figure of a ghost was once seen approaching the ladies toilet and was verbally apprehended by a customer. What is this attraction with toilets for Sussex ghosts, I can think of half-a-dozen instances; most unhealthy.

There is definitely an atmosphere at The Red Lion but it is far from an unpleasant one. I arrived on an unusually fine Spring day and the attractive trees, which make the inn almost impossible to photograph, had just had a haircut. I took my pint of strong ale out to the garden to converse with the chickens. Few pubs remain of The Red Lion's kudos, which is a sad loss to the character of old England.

HANGLETON MANOR INN
HOVE

Another inn named after a local manor house.

Hangleton to me is not Hove. It is a built up hamlet outside Hove. This being the case I cannot justify a description of Brighton's pleasant if over-shadowed neighbour.

Hangleton Manor originated in the 16TH century. Only to my untutored eye parts of it seem somewhat older. I was told that a part of it is now in private possession but this seems to me an unusual arrangement and I will not swear to its authenticity.

What is well-authenticated is that the old building began life as a hunting lodge and that several cottages that have long since disappeared surrounded it. Now unfortunately it is surrounded by a vast housing estate. It cannot be denied that this detracts from the ambience of the building.

The famous dovecote is still in existence and through scanning a local paper I discovered that it had been tastefully renovated in 1926. The builders work being so appreciated that it won an award. The paper also mentions that there were 520 nesting boxes contained within at the time of the renovation.

I visited Hangleton Manor Inn late in February 1999. I was staying at a hotel in Hove and the round taxi fare of £12 made it an expensive drink.

The front bar was comfortably furnished and quietly prestigious without emanating that vague snobbery that is perceived in some similar premises. Another main bar had been adopted by a birthday party, so I wandered through to a large back bar where I solicited the barmaid into a conversation about the supposed haunting.

"It's supposed to be a lady," she said. "She murdered her child and is meant to come looking for it. I've never seen her but I've heard the odd noise that has given me a bit of a fright."

She seemed to know little else, so I must therefore rely on rumour and legend.

The offending spirit here is that of a lady dressed in an expensive silk gown. She is thought to be a shade of a serving wench which makes her apparel a little strange to say the least. This maid, nicknamed Lady Jane by the current staff, is reputed to have been made pregnant by the resident Lord of the Manor. She gave birth but either through shame or lack of finances flung the tiny child to its death from an attic window. Other reports have the lady drowning the baby and then committing herself to the same fate. However, I deem this extremely unlikely.

There have been many accounts of this well-dressed maid over the years. Dogs find an upstairs room rather disconcerting and a ghostly pair of hands has been witnessed there. There has been a report at the inn of a young girl lying in bed who was approached by a spectral lady in white. She reported this to her mother. The mother had obviously heard the legend and advised her daughter, that should it happen again she was to say, "I am not the child you are looking for." We are informed that at a second occurrence the child uttered these words with success, the ghostly lady vanished.

Judy Middleton in her book Ghosts of Sussex informs us that a father saw a faint shape hovering over his daughter one night. She also tells us of a gentleman guest who was visiting from Wales. He had no knowledge of the history of Hangleton Manor but he was literally staggered by a vivid mental picture of a falling baby in swaddling clothes followed by a loud shriek.

What is strange about these cases is that various hauntings have been witnessed in several different rooms.

Let us assume that all the hauntings emit from the same unfortunate child.

Why the scream? Certainly not from the baby, it would not have known what was happening until it was to late. Possibly from the mother, if so it was for affect. She knew what she was doing. Possibly from another servant who saw the unfortunate accident, I don't know. Also I don't know how one gets a mental picture of a scream anyway.

Why is a servant girl dressed in an expensive silk dress? Perhaps the raunchy old Lord preferred his women that way. Perhaps whilst his wife was out the maid thought her mistress's clothing more becoming. Or, a little scarier, it was the mistress and not the maid that flung the inconvenient, illegitimate child to its death.

In nearby Hove the ardent ghost hunter might find the museum and art gallery worthy of some attention.

THE QUEENS HEAD
ICKLESHAM

Queens Head's are pretty well-known throughout the country. They represent any of a dozen regal ladies, the more popular being Elizabeth I and Victoria. There is the occasional comic reference to Anne Boleyn, who of course, lost hers. The unfortunate Queen was the inspiration for the several signs of "The Quiet Woman", the board depicting a headless one.

Icklesham is an attractive village twixt Hastings and Rye. The church is noted for it's Norman tower and knave. Nearby at Hog Hill is an 18TH century windmill.

The Queens Head is a little way off the main road but its situation on a lofty hill enables it to be seen from some distance. It is reported that from near the back door Dover's cliffs maybe sighted some 30 miles away.

The inn is half tiled and half bricked and began life as a farmhouse. Nearby a 12TH century manor was the site of some interesting archaeological digs; the whole area reeks of Iron Age man. Internally there is a massive fireplace almost surrounded by an inglenook. There are ancient beams but of a more modern situation there are collections of old beer bottles and farm implements. Where I instilled myself there was an unusual picture of Edward VII and a plaque in commemoration of a regular customer. John Major was the man's name but I hasten to add a man completely innocent of the political ambitions of his namesake. Major had been a regular at The Queens Head for much of his eighty years from 1917 to 1997.

An ex-landlord is the ghostly visitor at The Queens Head. George Gutsell was such a popular host that his coffin was laid on the bar counter whilst his regulars drank a final farewell. George died in 1890 at the age of 70.

It is possible that the deceased landlord was so touched by his send off that he decided not to go. At one stage, George made so many spirited farewell performances his favourite chair was made ready with a whisky beside it. The old innkeeper was always dressed the same. Described as portly with sideburns, beard and a moustache; he was attired in shirtsleeves, waistcoat and goldwatch and chain on a regular basis.

There is however a rather strange little story of a woman visitor who noticed an old man by the bar who disappeared when the lights came on. On hearing of this the regulars surmised that old George had put in yet another appearance. Going into detail they found the lady's description to be nothing like the spirited innkeeper. It was more in keeping with a smocked shepherd. Who knows? Perhaps old George is drumming up trade the other side of the veil.

ROBIN HOOD
ICKLESHAM

Legend has been even kinder to Robin Hood than it has Dick Turpin. There are at least 300 such signs in the country.

Landlords took Robin to their hearts insinuating that theirs was the type of establishment that aided the poor and needy.

Little is actually known of Robin Hood, he is thought to have been a 12TH century outlaw who frequented Sherwood Forest and Barnsdale, Yorkshire. Robin did not receive any attention for some three hundred years until Wynkyn de Worde put him in a ballad in 1490. He then achieved massive popularity. There are a hundred stories told about him and not a grain of truth in any of them.

Very rarely on inn boards Robin is accompanied by Little John.

The Robin Hood at Icklesham is a small local's pub on the main Hastings road. The interior is narrow but there are all the signs here of a good local patronage as well as a regular passing trade.

Unfortunately the import of pétanque has affected this region and the Robin Hood seems sadly afflicted. Why didn't the French play sensible games like Aunt Sally or cricket?

The Robin Hood isn't exactly haunted but a very nearby pond is. Andrew Green quotes residents as saying that it "emits a feeling of great dread or even evil."

The only visibly evidence is the spectre of a soldier in World War I uniform that glides backwards and forwards across the road. The soldier's route takes in the veranda of the Robin Hood; thereby justifying it's tenuous inclusion in this book.

SHELLEYS HOTEL
LEWES

Lewes is the county town of East Sussex; its ancient buildings bestriding the River Ouse. The castle is of Norman origin and the Barbican House contains a museum. Saint John's Church has an engraved stone that covers the grave of one of William the Conqueror daughters. A 16TH century house belonging to Anne of Cleves may be found in Southover and there are some fine 18TH century houses in Keere Street. The remains of Saint Pancras Priory survive as does the 18TH century market tower.

Famous people associated with Lewes include John Evelyn the diarist, Thomas Paine the pamphleteer and Doctor Gideon Mantell the palaeontologist.

There was an avalanche here in 1836, which killed numerous local people. A battle took place at Lewes in 1264 when Simon de Montfort defeated Henry III. Lewes is also famous for its massive firework display on November 5TH. It also has a prison and an obelisk to local martyrs on Cliffe Hill.

Shelley's Hotel began life as The Vine in the 1520's. The original sign depicted jolly Bacchus sitting on a wine cask and refilling his goblet. This signboard may still be seen in the Anne of Cleves house museum. The building remained The Vine until 1663 when the owner, the Earl of Dorset sold the building to the Shelley family. The celebrated Percy Bysshe being a member of this branch of the family.

In the 18TH century, probably due to the growth of the coaching trade, the house was enlarged. It can still be traced where the Elizabethan and Georgian structures meet. On a bedroom wall the builders discovered a 16TH century fresco, extremely well-preserved. In theme with the house the painting depicts Bacchanalian revellers with entwined grapes and flowers.

From 1800-1875 the house belonged to John Hodgkin. A chart in the resident's lounge shows the heights of the Hodgkin children while they were growing. During the First World War injured officers were housed in the building which had been utilised as a hospital. Later, the house was converted into two flats, until in 1932 Shelleys became a hotel. On the west side of the rear garden a new wing was built as the hotel gained in popularity. Shelley's remained in private hands until 1977. At that time it was purchased by Mount Charlotte Investments Limited.

I entered Shelleys on a fine March morning, almost unique in this country. As I was driving I constrained myself to a coffee. I was admiring a very large and detailed painting of a country scene when it arrived. The employee that brought the coffee was too busy for conversation but I did extract from him a few details of the haunting. I am afraid his knowledge was very scant indeed, so I am indebted to Guy Playfair who mentions it in his Haunted Pub Guide.

In room 26, in the 1930's, a guest committed suicide. His shade apparently lay dormant for several decades until in 1978 it surfaced with poltergeist activity. The unfortunate recipient of this inexplicable manifestation was a QC. Lying in bed this worthy gentleman of the law noticed that the scene outside his window was changing very slightly. The explanation was that his bed had risen by about three inches (there must be a jest here about taking his casement to a higher court but I can't think of one). Be that as it may this was the beginning of several examples of mild poltergeist activity in the room. As far as I can ascertain the activity ceased as abruptly as it had started.

There have been several other apparitions in various parts of the hotel but none of them appertaining to the unfortunate suicide. Here is a little known fact that will completely overwhelm the reader. There are more suicides in hotel bedrooms than anywhere else. More people opt for taking an overdose in unfamiliar surroundings than any other form of self-destruction. I know of a vast hotel in London that averages half a dozen suicides each year.

This being the case I should imagine that even the smart and tranquil Shelleys has experienced more than one suicide. If so, perhaps the QC's experience in room 26 is coincidental. It would seem to me that 40 years is an awful long time for a ghost to surface even in a dimension where time stands still.

Ghost hunters in Lewes should seek out the Anne of Cleves House museum in Southover. Reputedly there is a unique haunted table there, a tapping, leaping, juddering haunted table.

At nearby Grange Gardens a tourist took a picture of some floods. When the photograph was developed it showed the apparition of a man carrying an unknown object on his back.

THE BULL INN
NEWICK, Near LEWES

The sign of the bull has several explanations. One is that it represents the roast beef of old England. A far more likely explanation is that it relates to the terrible and inhuman act of bull baiting that was once a national 'sport'. Every town owned a post with a heavy metal ring to which the bull was attached. Local pubs obviously took up the name, hence, The Bull. Thankfully these torturous and barbaric exhibitions were finally outlawed in 1836.

Yet a third explanation of the sign of the bull is that it was derived from 'La Boule' the seal of a monastery or collegiate body. A fourth interpretation is that the beast was popular on many coats of arms and therefore taken on by local hostelries. Uniquely, at Newick, we have a fifth interpretation. The original sign at this inn represented the papal bull and bore the insignia of the seal of Rome.

Newick is a picturesque village on the fringe of the Ashdown Forest. It is roughly midway along the Pilgrims route from Winchester to Canterbury. Therefore Newick's geographical situation necessitated that there be several hostelries at this most natural of stopping off points. Such a hostelry is The Bull.

The Bull was established in 1510 just after Henry VIII was crowned. There have been many changes over the centuries but all have been tasteful and heeded the ambience of the building. One vast extension was added as early as the late 16TH century. Little has changed today, the four ceilings with their ancient beams are held in place by numerous original oak pillars. Adjoining the bar is a large restaurant, occupying the site of an old milking parlour.

The Bull needs a thorough inspection and the time to do it. There is something to catch the eye in every nook and cranny. There is a wonderful collection of bank notes adorning one wall and local events are advertised at the inn. When I was last at The Bull a 'Murder and Mystery Dinner' was being recommended.

Obviously there must be some type of ghost here. Such a well-organised establishment would not neglect such an essential detail. However, data is hard to establish. There have been reports of mild poltergeist activity over the years but the 'presence' is of a benign nature.

"Have you a resident ghost?" I enquired of the barmaid.

"We certainly have Sir," she replied "but none of us are sure who or what it is."

The would be ghost hunter will have to dig deep in Newick. If hauntings are akin to antiquity then there must be a dozen or so in the village. However, none of the villagers know or are prepared to talk of such things. It's frustrating.

HAYES ARMS HOTEL
NORTHIAM, EAST SUSSEX

The name of this hotel is a glorification of a local family, a not unusual practice.

Northiam has a 16TH century church with a tall tower and an unusual Sussex spire. An ancient oak on the village green is supposed to be the one under which Elizabeth I dined in August 1572. There are two great houses in the area; Great Dixter a timbered dwelling dating back to 1450 which has a splendid great hall and Brickwall with its 17TH century timbered front, which is now, a school.

The Hayes Arms is a 14TH century inn but was much added to in Georgian times. It now lets out attractive rooms with four poster beds and is often used by wedding guests staying over. The older part of the building boasts a large fireplace where Elizabeth I warmed her feet on journeys to Hastings or Rye.

The Hayes Arms has two unique spirits, both ladies. One is an old woman, benign of character who had connections with a spinning wheel that once stood in the bar. The spinning wheel has now gone and there is a strong probability that the old girl has departed with it.

The second lady is a little better known. It is thought that she is Molly Beale the daughter of a baker who once owned the premises. Poor Molly was murdered in her bed in the 1700's, but by whom we are not told. It is the unfortunate Molly, dressed in a grey cloak and large white hat that haunts the premises. Witnesses describe her as an attractive woman in her early thirties. As it was quiet and pouring with rain when I arrived I engaged the jovial landlord and his charming lady in conversation. They had only been at the hotel for a few months but had heard the legend of Molly Beale. They also told me of a cold spot in one of the upstairs bedrooms. What was news to me was that the landlord believed Molly to be a lady of horizontal entertainment, a lady of the nightlife, a purveyor of the oldest profession. He also suggested that she had been done to death by a customer.

This may be the case we shall never know. Far be it for yours truly to damage a lady's reputation, alive or dead (for three hundred years).

CROWN AND THISTLE
NORTHIAM

There are two explanations as to how the Crown and Thistle obtained its name. The first and most probable is that it celebrates the amalgamation of England and Scotland under one crown. The Rose and Thistle being a similar variation.

However, there is a second explanation. There is a slightly disparaging saying concerning our Scottish friends that states 'The finest thing a Scot can see is the road to the south'.

It is true that in the 17TH and 18TH centuries thousands of Scots came over the border to start businesses in England. Many took inns and amalgamated the separate symbols, hence Crown and Thistle, Rose and Thistle etc.

If one accepts this interpretation, one would expect the same of the Irish and Welsh who have both in their turn flooded into England. However, to the best of my knowledge there are no Rose and Shamrock signs and only one Crown and Leek, in Newtown on the Welsh border.

The Crown and Thistle at Northiam is reputed to be 14TH century; however, much has been added since. A lot of white weatherboarding, so much a trait of the Sussex and Kent builders, may still be seen.

Internally the owners are trying to keep the old fashioned charm of the building whilst being forced to keep up with financially mandatory modern times. A West Ham poster is on view and a karaoke is advertised. Another example of refinement and good taste is a pair of plaster feet poking out of a flowerpot, underneath is a sign 'Grow your own dope, plant a man'.

There are two resident ghosts at the Crown and Thistle, neither seen on a regular basis. One is a middle-aged woman in a long dark dress and antiquated bonnet. The other is reputed to dress in doublet and hose with a feather adorning his hat. There is little else to say.

PS The purposeful ghost hunter in Northiam should drop into the local church. He might be lucky enough to hear voices coming from the empty vestry.

HORSE AND CART INN
PEASMARSH

Obviously the Horse and Cart celebrates the necessities of farming folk. Once upon a time everything on the farm from hay to fertiliser to farmhands was transported by horse and cart. A unique and far more romantic similar sign could be seen on the Great North Road. It shows, or showed, a group of farmworkers at the end of the day. The inn's sign 'Wait for the Wagon'.

Peasmarsh is a border village where Kent meets Sussex. Hop and oast house country is this. The proliferal of the 'Garden of England'. A meandering long village is Peasmarsh, on the road to Rye. It has a smattering of interesting pubs one of which is the Horse and Cart Inn.
I pulled into the Horse and Cart at eleven o'clock one morning. I was surprised at the length of the building. There is quite a narrow frontage but once inside one notices the length of the dining area which must have been extended at least once. A vast wood burning stove sits majestically in the centre of the dining room. Everything is neat and homely which could be the reason for the 'Best Pub in Sussex 1991' sign that is proudly if not ostentatiously displayed in the front bar.
The Horse and Cart has what we in the trade call a nudger, a mild example of poltergeist activity. The attractive landlady calls it a pincher, a bum-pincher to be exact. I have no doubt whatsoever that she is sincere. In between seeing to the kids, preparing the bar and filling the tills with change, she looked me straight in the eye and told me that the unseen phantom has pinched her rear on numerous occasions. The perpetrator of these spirited assaults is one Harry the footman. Apparently he once lived in the old stables that subsequently became part of the dining area. Perhaps beyond the curtain an ancient footman still appreciates the rump of a young filly.

THE RINGMER INN
RINGMER, EAST SUSSEX

The Ringmer Inn is another board that reflects the situation of the hostelry. There are over 600 pubs in England that are named directly after their villages. The idea was to show that this particular inn was the most important in the village. As often as not however it was the only pub there.

Ringmer is associated with Gilbert White, the great clergyman, naturalist and author. White lived here at Delves House. Ringmer however stands very much in the shadow of Selborne in Hampshire. A village of which White wrote a history (*Natural History and Antiquities of Selborne*) which became world famous and is still selling in thousands today. Not to be totally outshone by its Hampshire rival, Ringmer makes much of a local tortoise that is mentioned in White's diary. So revered is the beast that it and the naturalist are to be seen on the colourful village sign. Various local dignitaries of lesser esteem share the same sign.

The Ringmer Inn was the victim of much poltergeist activity in the late seventies. This was no inept and obscure tapping and rapping this was your ghostly full monty. Lights turned themselves off and on again, heavy locked doors flew open, bottles leapt from shelves and there was a sound of a 14lb hammer smiting the walls.

This unknown poltergeist would appear to have been 'All mouth and no do' for when a team of researchers spent the night at the inn he ceased to function. Never again to darken the respectable inn's doorstep. Unfortunately The Ringmer Inn no longer exists. After several enquiries I was directed to the site which is now a block of flats. Try as I might I could find no reference whatsoever to any other haunting in Ringmer. I chatted in three of the local pubs but to no avail. Any would be ghost hunter will be wasting his time here. But, the village is pretty and well-worth a visit.

THE GEORGE
ROBERTSBRIDGE

Some Georges originated as Saint George and the Dragon. Later they were abbreviated to The George and Dragon until finally through economy of speech their mythical partner was dropped and just The George remained.

There are however many such signs that commemorate any one of our six kings of that name. Of these George IV is by far the most popular.

The village of Robertsbridge is an old staging stop and looks every inch of it. Robertsbridge straddles the River Rother and enhances it with a plethora of ancient houses and old inns. Slightly to the east of the village, near the appropriately named Abbey Farm, once stood an ancient abbey. There is now little to be seen of the building that has slowly been eroded by time.

The George is an old coaching inn but it has been greatly and tastefully modernised. There remains however a list of the landlords since 1484 and a tribute to Hilaire Belloc. Belloc the famous Sussex poet visited The George on several occasions. I wonder what he would have thought of the lyrics coming from a Sky pop programme in the larger bar on my last visit.

The ghost of The George is heard but not seen. It is a rumbling or juddering noise coming from a large room above the bars that is used for weddings and other functions. The noise is unusual in the fact that it is generally heard at lunchtime. Speculators suggest that it is a confirmed bachelor who objects to the room being used as a wedding reception venue: pure speculation.

SEVEN STARS INN
ROBERTSBRIDGE, EAST SUSSEX

The sign of the seven stars was very popular in the Middle Ages and some of the hostelries bearing this name today may trace their pedigrees back to that time. The board represented the seven starred crown invariably depicted on the head of the Virgin Mary. Later 'Seven Stars' are thought to have an astrological significance, the stars showing the constellation of the Plough. In turn this was to help travellers obtain their bearings. It seems ironic that I have seen several pubs of this name with a 'No Travellers' sign affixed to the door.

It would be inappropriate of me to try to add to the expoundings of such aristocrats of ghostwriters as Hallam, Green and Playfair all of whom have written at length on the Seven Stars, as of course have a greater number of lesser decree. However, as it is my intention to mention every supposedly haunted inn in Sussex I shall brook no defaulters. So much is known that it is better that I tabulate the reports. Firstly though, a comment on my most recent visit. Nothing seems to have changed in time immemorial here. A cassocked plaster monk gazes through a window, a red cross knight in full armour stands in the corner and a massive log in a huge fireplace still threatens to roll across the carpet. Did I say no change? There is one, a poster advertising a live band to appear in the near future. Nothing is perfect.

Now a brief if slightly speculative history of the Seven Stars Inn.

The Seven Stars was constructed in 1380 some 170 years after the nearby Abbey. There are reputedly two tunnels. One to the one time site of the Cistercian chapel now the foundation of the George Hotel. A second subterranean passage is thought to connect with an arched entrance some 500 yards to the south. I am led to believe that both tunnels have now been blocked, but in living memory exploration was attempted by two local stalwarts; lack of air made them turn back after a few yards.

Upstairs at the Seven Stars Inn is a room reputedly inhabited by Charles II during his captivity. There is also a passageway where a Franciscan monk, Brother Andrew, is said to have been hacked to death by Cromwell's roundheads. A strange construction at the Inn is a 70 feet shaft running from the attic to the cellar. The purpose of which is unknown.

The ghosts.

Firstly we have Brother Andrew, known as the Red Monk. The description coming from the russet colour of his order. He is described as a tall man with a white beard. Brother Andrew is probably the monk who met such a horrendous death at the hands of the parliamentarians. One of the more graphic incidents was described by an 18 year old female Canadian visitor in 1972. She described the spectral monk whilst knowing nothing of his history.

There have been numerous spiritual walkings and rumblings near Charles II's bedroom. Whether this is the royal personage (incidentally the black boy on many inn signs) or Brother Andrew one can only speculate. This ghost is never seen but it had a very daunting affect on one previous landlord's two Labrador dogs. It later made a similar impression on another ex-landlord's collie.

We have no idea what spiritual nasty put two police officers to flight one night. They were staying at the Seven Stars but spent most of the evening under blankets or tablecloths. Could it have been the unknown something that shook a naval officer awake twice in one evening. The officer was staying over as a caretaker for an absent landlord friend.

Let us finish with the poltergeist activity over many years. The following list is not in chronological order.

Gas taps and barrels have been turned on.

An empty lager barrel has been thrown across the cellar and on the same occasion 300 empty bottles were tipped out of crates.

At a separate time 28 cups were broken and shortly afterwards a barman was hit on the shoulder by a menu board.

One particular landlady had an awful lot of trouble with a shelf that expelled everything placed upon it with great gusto. This unfortunate woman also had great holes cut in her household sheets.

Finally, Guy Playfair had a semi-inexplicable incident with a loaf of bread.

I think that's all.

Ghost hunters in Robertsbridge might be interested in a cottage in Busheygate, a couple of white shapes have been witnessed here and there is an inexplicable smell of pipe tobacco.

THE KINGS ARMS
ROTHERFIELD, EAST SUSSEX

The sign of the Kings Arms has much the same explanation as the Kings Head. It is once again the case of a landlord doffing his cap to royalty.

Rotherfield, lofty country this, the village is situated at an altitude of over 500 feet. It has a fine church with a shingled spire, and as the name suggests, stands near the source of the River Rother. The village is justly proud of a one-time inhabitant Doctor Sophia Jex-Blake who became the first lady doctor in 1877 and spent the last twelve years of her life at Rotherfield.

The Kings Arms has been known to be haunted since the early 1950's. In those days an ex-England test cricketer, Maurice Tate, ran it. In 1952 the patter of tiny ghostly footsteps were first heard in one of the upstairs bedrooms. The footsteps were described as scampering or the sound of a child running swiftly.

Maurice's wife Kay first heard the phantom footfalls a year later whilst she was sitting downstairs with members of her family. Thinking it to be intruders they rushed upstairs, but needless to say the rooms were empty.

A pattern seemed to be developing when a new landlord took over in 1954. The footsteps were heard again on a specific day in June. This coincided with the events of two years previous. The following year (1955) a vigil was set up on the appointed day. Nothing happened, it never does. Personally I remember sitting all night at a house in Southwold where a little old lady was to appear on a specific day of the year. It was against my better judgement, nothing happened and I have never been tempted to do it again.

The fleeting footsteps at The King's Arms are purported to be those of a previous owner's young daughter. There is no evidence whatsoever to support this theory. It is merely a convenience born out of likelihood.

There have also been reports at the inn of a phantom nudger. I have had tenuous experiences with these spirits and they are very disconcerting. The one at The Kings Arms is inclined to tap an unsuspecting victim on the shoulder. Such actions are usually combined with a sharp drop in temperature.

I dropped into The Kings Arms one morning and sat in the garden in the company of an enormous concrete dog. I chatted to two locals who seemed to know plenty about the village. I brought the conversation around from pubs in general, to hotels, to the exorbitant price of rooms, to availability of rooms at The Kings Arms and finally to haunted bedrooms.

"There was a haunted bedroom upstairs," said one of my companions.

"Yes, it had a perpetual cold patch," rejoined the other.

Realising that my two companions knew little more than I, I let the conversation drop.

There is not much left to say about The Kings Arms other than my own fanciful and extremely unlikely theory.

What is not generally known is that a miller once hanged himself in The Kings Arms. Is it just possible that the scampering footsteps are those of his young daughter who is thought to have discovered the body. I mentioned it was fanciful.

Battle of Waterloo, Brighton
With its ghostly visitor to the toilets.

The Ram at Firle
A female basket maker with a badly
deformed leg haunts The Ram.

The Red Lion, Hooe
Haunted by an ex-landlord and the sound of a tobacco mill.

The Queens Head, Icklesham
Where spirits were put out for the deceased landlord.

The Hayes Arms Hotel, Northiam

Haunted by a lady at a spinning wheel, and Molly Beale,
a landlord's daughter with another possible profession.

Seven Stars Inn, Robertsbridge

Spectres include a red monk, Charles II, a
poltergeist and a terrifying something.

The Mermaid Inn, Rye
A perfect setting for its numerous spirits.

The Roebuck, Wych Cross
Where staff tolerate the odd spectre.

Oak Inn, Ardingley
Strange occurrences in the car park.

Spread Eagle Hotel, Midhurst
Unexplained tapping.

The Lion, Nyetimber
Landlady locked in bedroom.

The Star, Rusper
Phantom Lady has a favourite stool.

The Druids Head, Brighton
A cowled figure and a lady in red haunt here.

The Stag, Hastings
Dehydrated cats and ghostly highwaymen haunt the stag.

MERMAID INN
RYE

The Mermaid is a popular sign at seaports. Unlike The Ship and The
Anchor which have wandered far inland, this sign seems to stay near
coastal waters. Credulous sailors in the olden days believed in an
attractive blond who was half fish, usually seen holding a looking
glass in one hand and a comb in the other. It seems to me ironic, the
popularity of the mermaid amongst superstitious sailors, as the
sighting of one was a definite omen that your ship was coming to
grief.

Rye is an extremely picturesque town. It is ancient and looks it from
its cobbled streets to its 14TH century landgate. It was one of two
towns attached to the Cinque Ports. Rye now straddles the River
Rother and the River Tillingham; it's importance as a port having
diminished when the sea receded. Peacocks School associated with
Thackeray's Denis Duval dates from 1636. Stone House, Fletcher's
House, Lamb House and Old Hospital are all architecturally
noteworthy. There are also other notable buildings in Church Square,
High Street, Watchbell Street and Mermaid Street. Besides The
Mermaid Inn there are The Old Flashing Inn, The George, The Kings
Head, The Old Bell and The Pipemaker's Arms all of which are
steeped in history and well-worth a visit. Henry James lived in Rye
and the town is also associated with Sheila Kaye-Smith. The Ypres
Tower was once a prison there is also a rebuilt windmill and the Royal
Military Canal extends from the town towards the Kentish border at
Walland Marsh.
What can one say that hasn't been said a thousand times about The
Mermaid. It has adorned more books on Sussex than any other
subject. It is a chocolate box epitome of traditional Rye.
The Mermaid sits sedately above the cobblestones of steep and narrow
Mermaid Street. It is old, said to be from 1420. This might have been
the date of which the building originated but bits have been added
since, albeit as early as the late 15TH century. If the medieval, half-
timbered exterior with its famous iron sign is as attractive as a film
set, the interior is no disappointment either.
The crossbeams are rough-hewn complete trees. The panelling is
ancient and wafts of historical romance. The fireplace takes 6 feet
long glowing logs. It is said, probably without foundation, that the

chimney is so wide and high that one can see the stars in the middle of the day.

In Georgian times, when smuggling was an honoured profession in Rye, The Mermaid became the headquarters of The Hawkhurst Gang, a large and nefarious brotherhood. The old building afforded many hiding places for contraband, including a stairway leading to a secret passage and a cleverly concealed well.

Unexplained sightings of ghosts and spooks at The Mermaid are numerous indeed. I shall try to make some sort of order of these.

A	There is the inevitable grey lady who appeared at the foot of a bed. Her manifestation scared two guests so much that they ran into the living room where they spent the rest of the night.
B	There is also the grey lady who appears by the fireplace in Room 1. A side trick of this particular shade is to badly dampen any clothes left around. One wonders how. There is of course the strong possibility that ghosts A and B are one and the same lady moving around.
C	Ghost C is not visible, but he or she causes a physical depression on a bed in a certain bedroom. This invisible spirit could of course be another more wan manifestation of ghosts A or B or both.
D	Another invisible shade that flattens the cushions on a rocking chair. D may of course be another version of any of those mentioned above.
E	Is a female phantom of Room 15; again the same permutations may apply
F	They may also apply to F, who is a woman guest who doesn't answer to a cheery "Good morning."
G	Is certainly a separate ghost from those mentioned above (with of course the exceptions of C and D). G is of the male gender. He inhabits Room 10 and has a habit of walking through bathroom walls.
H	Is also a gentleman who inhabits bedroom 18 and dresses in old-fashioned clothes. He may of course be the same spirit as G but it seems unlikely. Once again there is the possibility of cross-referencing this gentleman with C and D.
I&J	Are completely separate from any mentioned above. They are a pair of duellists complete with doublet and hose that cross swords for some minutes in a predestined fight to the death. I finally slays J and deposits the body down a secret trapdoor

into what I have heard described as an oubliette (dungeon of death). Personally I treat the story of the duel with a healthy and incredulous scepticism.

THE GLOBE
RYE

The name, which is popular with the more mature establishments, generally commemorates the first circumnavigation of our globe. One would have thought in more modern times there might have been a propensity for naming pubs after mans first step on the moon. This however would not seem to be the case.

Retired sailors often took pubs and many used the sign of 'The Globe' to illustrate their previous wanderings. The inference to the public being you are dealing with a man of the world.

When entering Rye from the north, the sign of The Globe appears suddenly upon the left. It is not on the main road and this necessitates an abrupt u-turn on a hairpin bend or a trip into town before returning. I chose the former alternative. The inn nestles in the shade of a hill on the left of Military Road. More modern houses line the opposite side.

The Globe is ancient but has been tastefully modernised inside. It is a stonesthrow from the canal, which was a godsend to smugglers. Unfortunately the Council walled up as unsafe an underground tunnel that led from The Globe to the canal. It was supposedly specifically constructed for the transport of contraband.

The Globe's spectral lady in white is rarely seen now. It was once thought that she was concocted into existence by the smugglers. The idea being to scare off inquisitive townsfolk and so keep them away from the Globe's more nefarious activities. The logical opposition to this theory is that smuggling in Rye ceased a couple of centuries ago (or so we are told). The white lady has been seen at least twice since the war and on both occasions by unsuspecting customers.

The present landlord accepts the accounts as sincere but states that personally he has experienced nothing.

UNION INN
RYE

Union Inns generally commemorate one of two occasions, either the union of England and Scotland in 1707 or the union of Great Britain and Ireland in 1801. Similar commemorative boards are 'The Crown and Thistle' and 'The Rose and Thistle'.

The Union Inn is a neat little pub in East Street. It is originally 15TH century but has been altered internally to a lesser degree. During a renovation and the installation of central heating some bones were found in a wall. This was not an unusual practice in the past when unbaptised babies could not be interned in hallowed ground. What is unusual in this case is that the bones were thought to be those of a young girl and not a newborn child. One would have thought that there would have been time for a baptism before death. The only alternative that I can think of is that the poor child had some very contagious disease. There is of course the remote possibility of murder. We shall never know for sure, but for the more morbid amongst us the bones have been placed in a glass fronted case and set into a wall in the restaurant.

Obviously there is a ghost associated with the above mentioned macabre find. It is the spirit of a young golden haired girl who disappears through walls. Perhaps she was leading to where her remains lay to obtain a Christian burial. If so she has been denied this and might remain unfulfilled.

According to the barmaid I spoke to in July there is reputed to be a second ghost at The Union. This is the spirit of an unknown seafaring man.

Whether it was the golden haired waif or the old sailor who slammed the door in the face of a reporter in 1994 is not known. The young man was accompanying an investigative society looking into spirits at the time. Apparently they had been called in to discover the cause of an unusual smell.

So there you have one, two or maybe three ghosts, a box of bones, an unusual smell (now extinguished) and a slamming door. Incidentally, there has been a fairly recent fire here but there was nothing supernatural about that.

THE WHITE VINE HOTEL
RYE

The White Vine Hotel has adorned Rye's High Street since 1560. It was built as an inn but has been used, from time to time, as a private residence. Probably the most famous occupant was Charles Pix Meryon who became mayor in 1871. It was also the home of a famous local family named Holloway, who were known for their books on Rye and the surrounding district.

A pamphlet on The White Vine states that 'through the centuries the building has accumulated a Georgian façade which is adorned with established wisteria and lavish hanging baskets that reflect the season.' And very attractive it is too.
The trouble is that wonderful old places such as The White Vine are a mecca for disgorging coaches. I have nothing against the elderly, in fact I am going that way myself. But to stand behind forty or fifty OAP's who are deciding what to have in their sandwiches and the strength of their tea drives me to distraction. One can write off the best part of a day.
Back to The White Vine Hotel. It has experienced a type of mild and playful poltergeist phenomena. Pillowcases have been removed from the beds and in the kitchen, were the majority of activity occurs, vegetables have been mixed, sugar has been poured onto potatoes and flour sacks have been interfered with.
Taking the unusual opportunity of talking to the manageress I was also informed that an American guest has seen a white lady in her bedroom. Another guest had the feeling of being watched.
A university team from Canterbury went over the White Vine with specialised equipment. (Don't they always, Rye must have been a godsend for the overspecialised). Anyway the outcome was, they found some cold spots!

Rye is a veritable feast for the would-be ghost hunter. Here briefly is what is on the menu.
We have a host of spectral ladies. Two walk together in Mermaid Street wearing long dresses and crinolines. Another lady who haunts nearby disturbs watchers by passing through walls. There is also the lady who reputedly searches for her lost pearls. After bombing damage in World War II a helper found the pearls and gave them to

his daughter thinking they were beads. The Old Tuck Shoppe in Market Street had a spectral lady in grey and Lamb House in West Street has a little old lady who sits by the door. This one is a very benign spirit and thought to be the shade of a one time worker.

The males of the spirit world are not to be denied in Rye, they are just as numerous as their female counterparts and probably more frightening. We have John Breed's ghost that supposedly haunts two sites in the town. Breed was a butcher who murdered the mayor's brother-in-law in 1742(43). Apparently it was a case of mistaken identity! Breed knifed the wrong man. The butcher was hanged; the gibbet cage and his skull were exhibited at the Town Hall for a number of years. Incidentally, Breed's other bones were smashed and made into soup as a cure for rheumatism. Breed's ghost is said to haunt the Town Hall and the local Tourist Information Office.

An equally famous ghost is Brother Cantata; an unfortunate young monk who fell for a novice nun named Amanda. They were caught fleeing the town. It is not known what happened to the young nun, no doubt something extremely unpleasant. Brother Cantata was walled up alive and died a short while later. He had gone mad in the close captivity. Amanda had first been attracted by the monk's fine voice but since his terrible incarceration he could only make noises like a gobbling turkey. Brother Cantata's ghost may occasionally be seen in the appropriately named Turkey Cock Lane, but one is more likely to hear an uncanny gobbling noise.

There are supposedly a group of black monks moving across the chapel gardens who are described as sinister and extremely frightening. Fletcher's House has two ghosts, both males. Visitors have been met on the stairs by a young man in an Edwardian suit. The same location is also frequented by an old man dressed in top hat and tails. A very benign old ghost of a shepherd compete with smock haunts Gibbet Marsh and a rather timid little boy dressed in white used to visit the owner of a house in Watchbell Street.

Heard but not seen is a poltergeist at a local guesthouse that answers to 'Charlie' and haunted footsteps follow and then pass you in Needles Passage

I think that is everybody, good hunting.

THE WISHING TREE INN
SAINT LEONARDS, EAST SUSSEX

This sign is a one off, a unique reference to a tree planted by two sisters who lived here before it became licensed premises. One sister, a joker, of whom we shall hear more later, ordained the tree with the power to grant wishes.

Geographically Saint Leonards is now part of Hastings but it began life as a resort in it's own right. The architect James Burton and his son Decimus laid out the town in 1828 around a picturesque little valley that meandered down to the shore. Burton seemed infatuated with strange names, his plan included such as Mercatoria (The Market Square) and Lavatoria Square (where the washerwomen lived). Much of the architects buildings still survive and the valley is now an attractive public garden.

Hollington, once a village in it's own right is now virtually a part of Saint Leonards and therefore part of Hastings.

The Wishing Tree, a much altered pub, stands on the edge of a vast housing estate. It was once a private house owned by the two aforementioned elderly and affluent sisters. One of these is reputed to have been the practical joker, a vocation that would have been almost unique amongst the straight-laced Victorian aristocracy.

One or maybe both of the sisters have been seen in spiritual form at or near The Wishing Tree. Over the years, spectral old ladies dressed in black or grey have been noticed in the bars, the cellar, and, would you believe it, once again in the toilet.

One of these benign old dears, obviously the joker has been known to pull funny faces, a most unusual occupation for a ghost but not an unbecoming one. Less enchanting is the habit of one of these ladies to appear with a pram beside the road and then walk out directly in the path of an oncoming car. The greatly perplexed motorist screeches to a halt only to find no one around. It takes a special sense of humour to appreciate this kind of practical joke.

Unfortunately today there seems little of the romantic Victorian period surrounding The Wishing Tree. There is one large tree close to the pub but I doubt it is the one that granted wishes. It was also impossible to verify the existence of the two mischievous ladies. Here is a story that I have heard yet cannot in the least substantiate.

One sister would engage a company of other high bred Victorian ladies in conversation. She would tell them of the mystic properties of the large tree in the garden. A wonderful tree this, that could grant your greatest wish, if you were to stand in some ridiculous posture and pour out your innermost soul. Naïve to the point of gullibility many of the susceptible young ladies would walk to the tree, create a ridiculous pose, pour out their soul and make their wish. Nine times out of ten the desire would be that some handsome and wealthy gentleman might seek their hand. Imagine the amusement of the second sister skilfully hidden in the branches. I bet she nearly fell off of her perch. Imagine the amusement (and power) she would have knowing society ladies innermost secrets.

That's the story anyway.

THE ROYAL VICTORIA HOTEL
SAINT LEONARDS

The name of this hotel is obviously in honour of, and its patronage by, Queen Victoria.

Built in 1828 this is style and elegance at its best. The ambience of such places always makes one feel good. The sea terrace restaurant, the marble columns, the piano lounge and bar all add to the atmosphere.

I ordered a scotch and ice from an immaculate barman. "Will that be a gentleman's measure?" he enquired. "It certainly will," I replied and sank into a plush armchair and watched the world walk by on the promenade below.

I later enquired of a passing waiter if the ghost or ghosts still lodged here. He told me that he had never seen or heard anything but repeated the oft-told story. The ghosts of The Royal Victoria were a man and his dog. Legend dictates that the place caught fire many years ago. The manager was intent on some business and did not notice the extent of the blaze. He became entrapped and perished in the blaze along with his faithful dog that would not leave him. Both man and dog haunted the hotel for a number of years. They were mostly witnessed by the lift and blamed for it's mechanical failures. Put forward as a reason for the situation of the spectral pair, was the fact that the lift had once been part of the room in which the man and his loyal dog had perished.

Unfortunately for the dear departed canine loyalty seems to be a one way emotion. His master has moved on and left the poor animal to haunt alone. The dog had been seen fairly recently but the manager seems to have found peace some years ago. Perhaps the spectral mournful mutt still seeks his master as he did whilst this side of the great divide.

Whilst in Saint Leonards the keen ghost hunter should travel up Queensway towards the ridge. It is supposedly haunted by a person on a horse that makes no sound and leaves no hoofprints. Also in Saint Leonards Forest a dragon was slain and where it bled lilies of the valley grow. When was this mighty monster slain? The Middle Ages! No 1850. You would have thought that it would at least of got a mention in the local papers. NO.

NEW INN
SIDLEY, Near BEXHILL, EAST SUSSEX

The sign of the New Inn is self explanatory; it shows often that a hostelry has originated either as the only one in the area or alongside an older establishment. In turn, New Inn's, of which there are over 500, become the older establishment. The New Inn at Gloucester dates back to the 1450's.

Sidley has all but been engulfed by Bexhill, but try driving from one to the other on a Sunday when there is a car boot sale on. You will spend a frustrating hour or more in a traffic jam. If the New Inn did not have a ghost it would be necessary to invent one. It is the perfect setting, it is dark inside, there is an old fashioned inglenook and small rooms seem to go off at all angles. There is an atmosphere here that I have seldom felt in reputedly haunted houses. It is not a feeling of some forbidden force rather a sense of intriguing mystery.

I had heard of the usual phenomena associated with light poltergeist activity. Domestic appliances turning themselves off and on, doors opening and closing, the usual type of thing that occurs in *normal* haunted houses but which has much more scope for variation on licensed premises. I had heard of a lamp, a mist, footsteps that were heard by a reporter investigating the case and a phantom lady. How strange then, that when talking to locals and the barmaid I was told of something completely different.

According to the New Inns patrons the offending phantoms here are an old man and a small boy, assumed to be his grandson. No mention whatsoever of spiritual ladies or shapeless mists.

I spoke to the barmaid after dragging here away from a ribald battle of wits with her regulars. I asked her of the hauntings. "As far as I know," she said, "there are two. An old man and a little boy. I have never seen a sign of either of them but some of the older regulars have heard tales."

So there we have it, perm any two from half a dozen suspicious but far from proven sightings. Just before I left, the forthcoming barmaid did state that she hated being alone in the Inn late at night. She described the feeling of being watched, a very eerie feeling.

I am sure she is right, there is something at the New Inn. Even a cynical, insensitive and sometimes flippant writer such as myself can feel it.

THE QUEENS HEAD
WINCHELSEA, EAST SUSSEX

For an explanation of The Queen's Head please refer to the Icklesham entry.

Winchelsea with it's neighbour Rye were the two ancient towns attached to the original Cinque Ports. The old town of Winchelsea became submerged in the 13TH century. King Edward I rebuilt the town in 1283 above the River Brede's marshes.

What one first notices on entering this spick and span little town is the formal layout. The streets are in a gridiron pattern with all corners seeming to be at precise right angles.

Despite being sacked by the French on three occasions and being abandoned by a receding sea, three gates survive from the original walled town. The Strand gate being the most famous. Also worth seeing are the Alard Tombs, the Farnecomb Chantry, Greyfriars and the restored 14TH century Court Hall. Some of the older houses contain crypts that were once utilised as wine cellars. There is also an 18TH century restored windmill.

Hauntings at The Queen's Head are so flimsy and inept that I was in two minds as to whether to mention them at all. It boils down to a couple of insignificant and poorly attested 'things that go bump in the night'.

THE ROEBUCK
WYCH CROSS, EAST SUSSEX

The Roebuck is another very popular old sign. The roe deer is one of our oldest species, fossils having been found in the Cromer Forest bed. The popularity of the roebuck as a sign is not in glorification of the beast but the enjoyment obtained from the hunting of it

Wych Cross is a village situated in the Ashdown Forest. Creepy country this, the Forest has always emanated an air of mystery. Its Wealden Ridges with their heathland and thousands of acres of undulating woodland add to the feeling of vague mystery. Streams appear and disappear at will and one is convinced that he is the discoverer of a chanced upon lonely lake. Ashdown, however is a misnomer, there are very few ash trees about but there is a plethora of oaks, elms, Scots pines, sweet chestnuts and hazel trees.

Wych Cross stands some 600 feet above sea level; it has attractive views and some interesting footpaths. I presume that it's name is derived from the Wych elm and not in reverence to a lady adorned with a pointed hat and straddling a broomstick.

The Roebuck stands on a crossroads in a village that seems to consist of a garden centre, a handful of cottages and The Roebuck itself.

A luxurious building is this with club like settees and deep carpets. Its various floors are on many levels, which always enhances a building. It originated in the reign of Charles I but there have been many tasteful extensions, the most recent being a block of bedrooms discretely hidden behind the building.

I ordered a coffee from a charming American lady who assured me that the coffee-pot was in continual use. I walked through several interesting rooms and ensconced myself on a sun-drenched patio, life seemed complete.

I must admit that up to this time I had no idea whom or what haunted The Roebuck. I had seen one line in a book many years before, which to the best of my memory stated 'The Roebuck is another hotel that the BTA (British Tourist Authority) considers haunted.'

There was nothing for it but to enquire from the immaculately dressed young man who I had paid for the coffee. "Yes Sir, we have a ghost, she's seen on a regular basis. She is a nun but I don't know what her story is."

I asked if he had seen the spectre.

"No, I thought I caught a glimpse once but I couldn't be sure. Some of the staff definitely have and several of the guests have mentioned her."

In answer to a further question, he stated that there was no specific room the nun had a habit for, she turned up all over the hotel. I don't believe there was an intended pun on the word habit.

So there you have it, a phantom lady with no known story.

HAUNTED INNS OF WEST SUSSEX

THE AMBERLEY CASTLE HOTEL	Amberley
THE OAK INN	Ardingly
THE NORFOLK ARMS	Arundel
THE QUEENS HEAD	Bolney
OLDE PUNCH HOUSE (ROYAL ARMS)	Chichester
THE CHICHESTER INN or CHI (Formerly THE CASTLE)	Chichester
THE GEORGE	Crawley
THE SHADES (Formerly HOGS HEAD)	Crawley
OCKENDEN MANOR HOTEL	Cuckfield
THE KINGS HEAD	Cuckfield
THE CROWN (now THE KUBA BAR)	East Grinstead
THE ROYAL OAK	East Lavant
SPREAD EAGLE HOTEL	Midhurst
THE LION	Nyetimber
THE ANGEL	Petworth
THE STAR	Rusper
THE CRAB AND LOBSTER	Sidlesham
THE WHITE HORSE	Storrington
HALF MOON	Warninglid

THE AMBERLEY CASTLE HOTEL
AMBERLEY

The name is obviously unique and the explanation equally obvious.

Amberley is a delightful patchwork quilt of varying periods and styles nestling beneath a great wooded bluff of the South Downs. The village is situated on the South Downs Way that makes it a must for hikers.
Amberley's ancient curios have been collected by the local landlord of The Black Horse Inn and have been placed in a small museum of Downland relics.
Saint Michael's Church dates back to 681 and has some interesting if faded 12TH century wall paintings.
Meandering around the village, to the south-face of the castle is the River Arun. It crosses a dangerous unstable area here, Amberley Wildbrooks. These marshes alternate between bog, stream or flood depending on current weather conditions. The trains and embankments built on such deceiving terrain were thought to be a wonder of construction in 1863.
Amberley Castle, now partially adapted to a hotel, was the summer palace of Bishop Luffa and other medieval Bishops of Chichester. It is still very impressive with its massive rocklike masonry. It is difficult to believe that such a building with its turrets and battlements was never intended to be a serious fortification.
I decided to visit the Amberley Castle Hotel after enjoying a drink in Storrington. I had heard, some time ago, a radio announcer describe it as 'the most romantic hotel in Britain.'
Taking an extremely tight right hand turn off the main road I saw the hotel in front of me. From several hundred yards away it appeared resplendent and romantic. Unfortunately there is a sign stating that the hotel is only open to guests and those that have made a previous appointment. I carried on regardless. Even a scruff like myself can enjoy a drink at the Ritz, Waldorf, Savoy or Dorchester with little or no embarrassment.
However, a little further on I cam across a notice that quite plainly assured one that your company was not accepted unless a prior appointment had been made. I retreated, terrified of boiling oil coming from the battlements, and not having time for a lengthy siege, carried on to Arundel.

In all the books I have written on ghosts and pubs, this is the only time I have failed to visit the site on which I am writing. I must therefore lay before the reader a précis of an account by Andrew Green, the greatest of all ghost hunters.

The spirit of Amberley Castle is that of a young serving girl named Emily. Poor Emily is thought to be only 14 and may well have been the victim of a bishop's lust. The sad shade of the young serving girl is reputed to haunt an area that was once the palace kitchen, just outside of the main walls. It is summarised, with very little evidence, that Emily either committed suicide after her encounter with the perverted bishop, or died of marsh fever that was prevalent at the time. Whatever the poor waif's fate, she has not been seen for sometime. Perhaps she finds it difficult to make an appointment.

PS Whilst in Amberley the avid ghost hunter might inquire into the two ghosts often seen at the Rectory. Incidentally, when a dining room cupboard was moved in 1904, two bodies were found beneath it.

THE OAK INN
ARDINGLY

In the case of The Oak at Ardingly, the board celebrates an oak opposite the Inn. However, I did not find the tree and the several others surrounding the inn were very unimpressive, not at all supreme examples of their species.

Ardingly is a pretty and functional village. It is home to the South of England Showground and the well-known public school Ardingly College. A mile and a quarter to the south-west of the village is the Grand Ouse Viaduct on the main Brighton railway line.

A similar distance to the north of the village there is a National Trust property Wakehurst Place. It is Elizabethan in origin and stands in 520 acres of woods, gardens and lakes. Wakehurst Place is open to the public and is administered by The Royal Botanical Gardens at Kew.

The Oak Inn is reputed to be as old as the tree opposite. This is confusing, as the building became an inn in 1628 but it's prior existence was that of a private dwelling. The Oak is all that you would expect from an ancient inn, low beams, shining brasswork and an inglenook. There is a story here concerning a one-time member of the local hunt that met at the pub. Apparently this man had a fine hunting horn which he took with him to France during the war. He often blew the horn to sound defiance in battle. The charm of the instrument would seem to have worked, for the villager returned with both body and horn intact. The instrument was placed behind the bar where it remained for many years.

The legend attached to The Oak Inn is that it was once three woodcutter's cottages not one. In one of these cottages lived a man who coveted a young widow that dwelt in another. The man was besotted. One day, being well in his cups, he could no longer resist temptation. Grabbing her and dragging her upstairs he bound her and then returned to his ale, obviously savouring the expectations of events to come.

The lady made an escape bid through the window, but got no further than the garden, where she was overtaken by the woodcutter who killed her in a drunken frenzy. As often is the case there is no date affixed to this terrible occurrence. There are no names for slayer or slain, no record of a trial and no indication as to what happened afterwards, to families or dependants.

What is better authenticated is that this unfortunate young woman still haunts the Inn. Yet again dressed in grey her spirit has been seen crossing the barroom from the rear of the house to the inglenook. She has also been witnessed sitting at the bar and even mistaken for a barmaid behind the counter. The lady is also thought to be responsible for a sharp dig in the back that one customer experienced whilst he was alone in the bar. Apparently this occurrence upset him so much that he has since refused to remain in the bar alone.

There has been, as always in these cases concerning pubs, a plethora of minute examples of supernatural interventions. Lights switching themselves on and off, beer taps turning themselves on, tankards behind the bar mysteriously swinging on their hooks etc. etc.

I had a drink with the relief landlady here one morning. She informed me, during our conversation on spooks, that she had done relief for 30 years. During that time she had relieved in 96 premises; the majority had been fine, several had had an atmosphere and two she would not enter again at any price.

Asked if she felt a *presence* at The Oak, she replied that there was a warm and friendly atmosphere but nothing else. She then called a barmaid of some longer standing and asked if she knew of the house ghost.

"Oh yes," she replied. "It is a lady in grey, who was murdered years ago. She hasn't been seen in the house for years but she frequents the car park and does all manner of mischief."

I know the feeling, a ghost in an Aldershot car park jacked up my mate's Rover and disappeared with two wheels.

But to return to The Oak. If this is the case it is unique. It is the first instance of a spirit changing it's venue that I've heard of.

Before leaving the relief landlady informed me "Try The Crown at East Grinstead, that's definitely haunted."

THE NORFOLK ARMS
ARUNDEL

This Hotel takes its name from the Dukes of Norfolk, Earls Marshal of England for 500 years. Arundel Castle is the family home.

Arundel Castle was originated in the reign of Edward the Confessor and completed by Roger Montgomery, Earl of Shrewsbury, after the Norman Conquest. Cromwell's troops destroyed most of the castle in 1643.

The castle was rebuilt in the 18TH century but the original keep and barbican were preserved. Today, it contains paintings by Van Dyke, a magnificent library and a fine collection of armour.

Arundel's parish church, Saint Nicholas's, is dated from 1380 and has now become the Fitzalan Chapel. Incidentally, it was from its tower that Cromwell bombarded the town. The cathedral of Our Lady and Saint Philip dates from 1868 and was designed by Joseph Hansom, the inventor of the Hansom cab.

A unique attraction of Arundel, and it must be said, not one suitable to all tastes, is the Museum of Curiosity. It shows the work of Victorian naturalist and taxidermist, Walter Potter. Potter has arranged a tableau of stuffed animals and birds.

The Norfolk Arms is an 18TH century coaching inn and looks every inch of it. The hotel stands proud yet unassuming at the bottom of the High Street. I arrived one Saturday morning. The hotel was, as I had previously feared, full of tourists. It was an inappropriate time to ask about any supernatural happenings. It was obvious that I would have to rely upon things that I'd heard and read previously.

Before describing the alleged supernatural happenings here I must remark upon a notice in the front bar. It states that 'Anyone seen using a mobile phone in the room will be accompanied by the sound of a bell behind the bar.' I glanced up to see a large ship's bell behind the counter. I should imagine that the ringing of such an implement in the background would make any attempted mobile telephone conversation null and void.

I had read about The Norfolk Arms ghost whilst searching for another story in The Worthing Herald. A lady working in the taproom in the 1980's witnessed a man, stripped to the waist, leap through the kitchen window into the yard. It is intriguing to learn that the window was not fitted until the 1950's. Shortly after the fitting, a face began to appear on the other side of the pane. There was also a considerable amount of poltergeist activity.

For those who like to have a cut and dry reason for their hauntings, there is a rumour that a murder occurred in a bedroom here in the 1800's. Boastfully I count myself as an expert on old and obscure murders in the south of England. I have literally dragged up hundreds from local papers going back to the1700's and have written three books on the subject.

I cannot find any reference whatsoever to a murder at The Norfolk Inn in the 1800's. However, this is not by any means proof that none occurred.

I once mentioned this particular haunting to a friend of mine in Chichester. He knew the case well and pointed out the man seen leaping through the window was the perpetrator of the crime making good his escape. It did not seem obvious to me.

Andrew Green tells us of a local town crier who has studied the case in depth. He also tells of the sound of a chain being pulled across gravel. How's this for a fanciful scenario. The murderer watches his unknown prey (face at the window). He later returns and puts his plan into affect. Killing he or she, the murderer pushes the body through a window (poltergeist activity). Disturbed, he leaps through the casement himself (jumping man). He returns late at night and drags away the body (sound of chains). He secretes the body and the crime goes unreported. Trouble is there was no window. Bit far fetched? Probably so.

Whilst in Arundel the avid ghost hunter should have a look around the castle. There are reportedly four spectres.

Bevis, a one time warden, who when dying cast his mighty sword and asked to be buried where it lay. A mound called Bevis's Grave marks the spot.

A young girl crossed in love, who threw herself from Hiorne's Tower. A cavalier, known as the blue man and a young kitchen scullion.

THE QUEENS HEAD
BOLNEY, WEST SUSSEX

For an explanation of The Queens Head, please refer to the Icklesham entry.

Bolney, this attractive and unassuming little village, has now been by-passed by speeding traffic. The A23 now skirts the hamlet leaving it once again to develop its character. Once several dozen coaches a day stopped to change horses and sustain their passengers on this main route from the capital to Brighton.

The Queens Head now stands a little gaunt and remote on the old A23. This is a little of a cheat as far as haunted pubs are concerned as the supernatural action took place outside.

The strange affair outside The Queens Head is a one off as far as I can ascertain. In the late 1980's a car was travelling along the A23 towards Brighton. The occupants decided it was time for a rest and proceeded to turn into The Queens Head car park. As the driver completed the manoeuvre, the figure of a lady suddenly appeared. A collision was inevitable. Not only did the passengers see the unfortunate woman struck; they also felt the physical impact. The strange thing was that the lady, dressed in grey, had disappeared when the men got out to inspect the result of the collision. The car's occupants had their version of events endorsed by two independent witnesses who stated categorically that they had seen a woman suddenly appear before the turning vehicle.

Police were called and an extensive search was mounted but to no avail. The lady had disappeared into the mists of the unexplained.

Considering the amount of carnage on our roads one would imagine there to be at least one unrested spirit for every mile of major road. There are in fact extremely few. There has been a mention of a lady in red on this same road near Handcross. I can also remember one being reported at Arborfield in Berkshire, but it was an extremely fanciful account.

There are of course a dozen accounts of the phantom hitchhiker. A kindly driver picks up a hitchhiker; they indulge in pleasant conversation and then the driver finds he is talking to an empty seat. Total balderdash of course. Anyone relating this popular story will never tell it in the first person. It will always have happened to a mate of his.

Slightly more believable is the spectre that appeared on a minor road running from Marlborough to Hungerford. Many years before a young boy had been killed falling from a frightened horse. A memorial stone had been placed there but had been dislodged when the road was widened. It was thought, that the man who appeared on numerous occasions was the long dead father looking for his son's memorial stone. Also there was a cluster of well-substantiated cases in 1952. The A3 between Esher and Cobham was the domain of a phantom that broke car windscreens with missiles. There was a vast amount of police activity but nobody, ghost or mortal, was ever brought to book.

Finally there is the female ghost that inhabits the old roadway at Bluebell Hill, between Maidstone and Chatham. This lady has been witnessed on so many occasions that one feels quite neglected if she does not put in an appearance.

OLDE PUNCH HOUSE (ROYAL ARMS)
CHICHESTER

The Olde Punch House got its name in appreciation of a very potent punch brewed on the premises. In fact the tipple was such a favourite of Queen Victoria that she granted the incumbents a Royal Warrant in 1840. In all probability this gave rise to the taverns other name of The Royal Arms.

Queen Victoria was not the first regal lady to visit the Olde Punch House. In 1591, when it was still a private residence, the owner, Lord Lumley, entertained Queen Elizabeth I here. The Elizabethan room with its splendid Italian plaster ceiling still exists in its original form.
The Olde Punch House became an inn in 1750 during the reign of George II. The license was granted to a Mr Weller who seems to have held it through many years and several reigns.
The Olde Punch House sits sedately in East Street not even a stones throw from the city cross. It has a bowed window façade with hanging hops leaves over the doorway. The interior has much of its original 16TH century oak panelling and beams and what is left of a walled garden can still be seen from the rear of the large bar room. The interior is inclined to be dark and some of the seats need a little reupholstery but in essence the atmosphere is congenial. Personally I have seldom missed a drink here on many visits to the town.
Do you not just detest the type of insincere person who claims to have *haunting feelings*, *vibes* and *senses of the paranormal* about certain places? Don't they just bore the backside off of you?
WELL!
I had *haunting feelings*, *vibes* and *senses of the paranormal* at the Olde Punch House long before I broached the subject. It was a warm evening in July and a young barmaid, a third of my age and with better legs, was enjoying a smoke at the door. I engaged her in conversation about the age of the pub, the clientele etc. etc. then subtly tossed in the comment "I suppose you haven't got a resident ghost?"
"Oh yes, in fact we have two," she replied "a lady and a man."
"Have you ever seen them," I enquired.
"I thought I saw the lady once but I'm not sure. Plenty of the other girls have, she is thought to be an ex-barmaid. The lady is benign but the man in the cellar is far more sinister. I hate going down there some

nights. You can feel his eyes boring into the back of your head. The Chichester Observer did a piece on it many years ago."

I thanked the young lady for her information and left. I had not then, nor since seen the write up in the local paper.

I sauntered slowly up the street, smugly congratulating myself on the accuracy of my *vibes.*

THE CHICHESTER INN or CHI
(Formerly THE CASTLE)
CHICHESTER, WEST SUSSEX

I had not been to this inn for years and was disappointed to see that it had changed its name. As I write in the late nineties it seems to be the fashion; a fashion that is not to be admired. There was nothing a matter with the previous name of 'The Castle'; it had served this particular pub well for hundreds of years as it has some 600 others about the country.

In general the sign of The Castle has an obvious explanation, it is out of respect or allegiance to any localised fortress or castellated manor. There are several within a stones throw of Chichester. May I humbly suggest, with no evidence at all, that as The Castle inn sits in close proximity of the towns ancient walls, it may once have been in the vicinity of some fortified building. I shall not insult the reader's intelligence by explaining that the present day sign 'The Chichester Inn' means an inn at Chichester

The easiest way to do a quick run down on the beautiful old town of Chichester is on a 'places to see' basis.

1. The Roman Regnum that preserves the site of the amphitheatre
2. The Norman cathedral with it's rebuilt spire
3. The yachting in Chichester harbour
4. West Gate House and Dodo House, both ascribed to Wren
5. The Bishop's Palace with it's notable chapel
6. Priory Park with it's remains of Greyfriars Monastery
7. 18TH century houses in Saint Martin's Square
8. Saint Olave's Church, a bookshop when I last visited
9. Saint Andrew's Church with the grave of William Collins, the poet
10. Saint Mary's Hospital Almshouses and Crawley Almshouses and much much more

Incidentally William Blake the great artist and poet was tried here for treason and acquitted

Now back to West Street and The Chichester Inn. All that I could really ascertain about the history of the old inn was that there had been some type of building here since the 12TH century. Tradition has it that the present building was once a smithy that developed into an inn. This is probably so in many cases, it was a natural progression. "Do you fancy a pint whilst I'm shoeing your horse?"

The Chichester Inn now stands near an extremely busy roundabout. I visited it during Christmas 1998, after doing some traditional shopping. It was lunchtime and I was pleased to see a genuine open fire in the front bar. The young bartender was polite and efficient but no the type I thought I could enquire of ghostly visits. As a famous ghost writer once explained 'One cannot really push ones way to the bar and say "Pint of bitter please and have you witnessed any spooks lately".' This being the case I must rely upon the traditional story.

The Chichester Inn is reputedly haunted by a centurion who marches from the inn along what is left of the Roman wall. He then proceeds around the cathedral and returns along the former wall to the pub. Surprisingly this particular spirit has been witnessed more times than one might think considering his venerable age and the now bustling environment. I can add little more other than the soldier's courage is beyond doubt. Imagine parading along the city walls in a centurion's mini-skirt with a south-westerly wind coming across from Chichester Harbour. It doesn't bare thinking about.

Whilst in Chichester the ghost hunter should search out an Elizabethan house in East Street. It was once visited by good Queen Bess and has experienced poltergeist activity ascribed to 'Percy'.

There is also a haunted gravestone in the cloisters of Chichester cathedral. It's cheerful message reads

> Thou wandering ghost
> Take home this rhyme
> Next grave that opens
> May be thine

THE GEORGE
HIGH STREET, CRAWLEY

For an explanation of The George sign please read the Robertsbridge entry.

Crawley, a 'new town', was intended to be the utopia of British planning and to a visiting layman like myself the authorities have got most things right. Driving down from Gatwick one passes through a mile high Silicon Valley. The old town seems tucked away in a corner. It seems as though its younger brother has exclaimed "I'm proud of you. I shall maintain you. Now please sit on the sideline and do not get in the way of progress."

Several years ago I was told that Crawley had the lowest unemployment of any town in the country. Obviously this brave boast was greatly aided by having Gatwick Airport on its doorstep. Every recreational activity is catered for in Crawley and I am told that Tilgate has three lakes: one for sailing, one for rowing and one for fishing.

The George stands on the High Street that was once the old A23, London to Brighton road. Its gallows sign has adorned the covers of several books on ancient hostelries. The inn was opened in 1615, but unfortunately, as with many other inns, much of its colourful history has gone unrecorded. It is known however that it was a favourite stopping place for the Prince Regent when travelling to and from Brighton whilst keeping an eye on the construction of the Royal Pavilion.

For many a traveller on the Brighton Road, The George's situation made it an ideal place for changing horses. It is also rumoured that the smuggling community found its cellars conducive for storage. It made a convenient overnight stopping place when transporting contraband from the coast to the capital.

My most recent visit to The George was in January 1998 and I was pleased to see that its venerable ghost was mentioned on a wall notice.

Soon after The George was built it employed a night watchman named Mark Hueston. Hueston stood six feet six inches tall, weighed 18 stones and patrolled the corridors armed with a pistol and a cutlass. His formidable presence acted as a deterrent to any potential burglar. One night a guest poisoned a bottle of wine that he kept by his bedside. The reason for this action was unclear. It has been suggested that wine had been disappearing from his room and that he took this rather Draconian step to deter the thief. Unbeknown to the guest, any leftovers of food or drink became one of Hueston's perks. It has been said that he plied guests with wine and vitals so that there would be a quantity of leftovers in the morning. One evening Hueston could not be aroused from his cubby-hole opposite bedroom seven, where he slept the day away. Staff later found the gentle giant dead from drinking the poisoned wine. An accident, he not being the intended victim

It is thought to be the night watchman's invisible spirit that is responsible for several shapeless manifestations and mild poltergeist activity at The George. Recently there has been a spate of lights going off and on of their own accord. There are also people who experience 'an uneasy feeling' in parts of the building.

THE SHADES (Formerly HOGS HEAD)
CRAWLEY

The sign of The Shades is not that unusual but its explanation is somewhat obscure. It is only recently that the board has appeared as an individual sign, for years it was dependent on a more splenderous building. For example, when the larger hotels finally decided that they needed working class money to help them stay solvent, they built small unobtrusive bars attached to the main buildings. There, locals could get noisily drunk as sacks without disturbing the more refined clientele. I can only hazard a guess that the name came about by being in the shade of the main building. It is not unusual to find in our older towns The Victoria Hotel Shades, The Premier Hotel Shades, The Royal Hotel Shades etc. etc.

The Shades at Crawley (once The Brewery Shades, then The Hogs Head, now once again The Shades) stands near the bottom of the High Street opposite the old Crawley market. It is in part 15TH century but so many changes have been wrought upon the old building it is difficult to ascertain which part. The Shades is not unattractive inside. It's varying floor levels and numerous alcoves give it an air of intrigue. There are several reported phantoms here. A grey lady and her child have been witnessed in an upstairs bedroom. Slightly disconcerting is that this is the same room in which the manager once slept. He opened the door one afternoon to find his bed inexplicably ablaze. Could this be the same spectral pyromaniac who leaves a pipe's aroma and ash in the ladies toilet? I am always a little suspicious of spirits that show signs of human weaknesses.
The final and most annoying phenomenon at The Shades is a recalcitrant doorbell. Ringing is heard at the most unfavourable of hours. The offensive bell jams itself on and refuses to be released.

When visiting Crawley, the ardent ghost hunter may find the time to take a pathway beside the railway line. If he is lucky, or possibly unlucky, he may come across the spectre of a 'putty faced' man. This ghost walks straight through the fencing to the railway line.

OCKENDEN MANOR HOTEL
CUCKFIELD

Cuckfield is a large thriving and expanding village. It is situated a couple of miles from Haywards Heath but has maintained its individuality. Many of its buildings date back to the Tudor period and are pleasing on the eye. Cuckfield has an almost unique situation between the noble South Downs and the mysterious Ashdown Forest. Elizabethan originated Cuckfield Park has a fine gatehouse and the remainder of the building has been utilised as a school. It was the inspiration of Harrison Ainsworth's *Rookwood*. Another author associated with Cuckfield was Henry Kingsley who died at Kingsley Cottage. Henry was the lesser-known brother of Charles.

Ockenden Manor dates from 1520 and as it's name dictates was once a manor house. The building abounds with tunnels, secret passageways and at least one priest's hole. There is also an original hidden chapel in the vicinity of one of the discovered priest's hideaways. I am told that all of the hotel bedrooms are called after members of the two families that have owned the establishment.

The interior of the Ockenden Manor Hotel is smart, elegant, stylish and plush. When bed and breakfast runs into three figures or more it is advisable to settle for just a drink. The bar I was shown into was small but tastefully decorated. There are some strange colourful glass birds decorating the panelled walls together with some fine pictures based on the adventures of Pickwick. I must also remark on the splendid toilets.

Unfortunately the ghost of Ockenden Manor is fading fast. Would you believe yet another spectral grey lady? Ockenden's grey lady is reputed to haunt the Raymond room and the landing outside the door. She has been noticeable by her absence of late but she was much in evidence in the 1980's when a honeymooning couple refused to stay in the room.

On another occasion, an elderly lady resident stayed in the room. In the morning she refused, point blank, to spend another night in there. The lady would give no reason but was adamant about her decision. Speculation based on probability dictates that she had had an altercation with the grey lady.

If time affects those beyond the veil as it does poor earthbound creatures, then perhaps this is the reason for this spectre becoming paler. She is not a shade of the shade she used to be.

THE KINGS HEAD
CUCKFIELD

For an explanation of this board please refer to the Hastings entry.

An ancient and attractive pub was this, with vast canopied doorways and ivy mantled walls. The female ghost that wandered its stairways and garden for many years was known affectionately as Geranium Jane. Jane was a local barmaid who became the paramour of the landlord. Jane became pregnant which made her an inconvenience. Nasty expensive things are children, especially when the mother can't work.

The landlord solved his dilemma by dropping a large geranium pot on Jane's head from a great height. A clever solution was this, as it not only killed two birds with one stone pot but it could, and was, interpreted as an accident. The ghost of Jane was quite terrifying as it was described as a running woman, silently screaming and covered with blood.

The reader has no doubt gleaned from the above paragraph, being in the past tense, that The King's Head no longer exists. I was told by a local that it is now a block of flats. What a crying shame. I visited the site but thought it pointless to inquire if Geranium Jane was still in residence.

Whilst in town, the eager ghost hunter should look up a property associated with the once great Sergison family. Several visitors here have met a lady on the stairs. When describing her to the residents, they have been met with an uninterested "You must have seen our ghost then."

Be careful, I believe the building is now a school and therefore not open to the public.

THE CROWN now THE KUBA BAR
EAST GRINSTEAD

The Crown was once the most popular sign in the country. Now however the ridiculous fad for trendy and mostly inexplicable names has sadly diminished the stalwart and respected boards. In early days pubs were often taken by ex-stewards and retainers of royal families. For this reason, and because the establishments were often on Crown Property, the symbol of the realm was often honoured. Without doubt the number of Crowns grew because of the increasing popularity of the royal family.

The Crown at East Grinstead was once a beautiful old inn at the centre of an attractive town. It is still a three-storey building that dates back to the 16TH century. It was visited by Oliver Cromwell, who was no doubt planning some nefarious schemes. Hanging Judge Jeffreys also used it as he toured the area handing out instance justice. I wonder what either of these awesome characters would say about the interior today.

I heard about the hauntings at The Crown from a landlady who had once done a relief there. She told me of mild poltergeist activity; the sort described as 'things that go bump in the night'. It was a bit of a woolly description badly lacking in detail.

Before leaving for East Grinstead I telephoned a friend who once lived there. He had heard of some vague haunting and said that if his memory served him well, he believed that it was associated with one of the bedrooms.

I arrived at East Grinstead on a rainy morning. I had forgotten what a terrible town it was to actually arrive at the centre of. Roadworks and traffic lights everywhere. I finally arrived with a sense of achievement but my troubles had only just started. I was misdirected three times to The Crown, which is not surprising considering it had changed its name. Then when I actually arrived there parking is another nightmare.

On entering one is greeted by the brilliant orange, yellow, peach and apricot colour scheme. The Kuba Bar is exactly what it says, an appreciation of Cuba. Fidel and Che look down from mirrors. The whole orientation is towards long orange cocktails ordered from extensive menus. Clean, popular and trendy it is, a pub it isn't.

I enjoyed a great bowl of coffee and struck up a conversation with a young barman. "I used to stay here in the eighties," I lied. "It used to have a reputation for being haunted."

"I 'ent never seen nothing," he replied.

End of conversation and inquiry.

It seemed pointless pursuing the matter as it was long ago and associated with a bedroom. The upstairs has now been converted into solicitor's offices. As a breed lawyers are an unimaginative body! Until your bill arrives, that is.

I have no idea if the Classic Cinema is still in East Grinstead, but the enthusiastic ghost hunter should enquire as to whether an ex-manager still haunts the site.

THE ROYAL OAK
EAST LAVANT

This sign at East Lavant celebrates, with some 1500 others, the national rejoicing over the restoration of Charles II to the throne. It identified the oak as a symbol of Charles's escape by hiding in an oak tree after the Battle of Worcester.

Lavant is a pretty village near the Hampshire border. It contains three pubs ands a semi-famous girl's school. East Lavant is separated from the rest of the village. It owes its existence to its situation. East Lavant was a convenient changing place for horses in the coaching era.

The history of The Royal Oak is a little obscure. It is one of those frustrating pubs that must have an extremely colourful history but little or nothing has been recorded. It owes its present popularity to the close proximity of Goodwood and Chichester.

The Royal Oak is an inn that reflects the weather conditions with its own ambience and atmosphere.

When I first arrived at the inn some years ago it was a beautiful summers day. The old pub seemed to glow with the reflected sunlight and seemed benign and welcoming. My second visit was quite the reverse, there is very little street lighting in East Lavant, it was 9:30 p.m. on a November evening and it was raining cats and dogs. I was drenched in the few seconds it takes to run from the unique horse shoe car park across the road to the building.

It was a night that would leave little doubt in one's mind that all the terrible tales that were told of the inn were accurate to a word.

My third visit was on a grey day just before Christmas 1998. The atmosphere was friendly and a Yuletide table was set out in the dining room. I took my regular large scotch with a pint of bitter chaser and sat under a massive wooden propeller and studied the picture of an ancient Ferrari. Perfect peace.

However, The Royal Oaks history is far from peaceful. It is said to have been the scene of much smuggling activity in the 18TH and 19TH centuries. In those days money was a necessity for survival and life was cheap. Two smugglers caught in the act by a couple of custom's men did them to death on the spot. The bootleggers were soon caught in a small village like Lavant. They were hanged near the spot as a warning to others.

A slim man with a head covered by a spotted neckerchief and sporting a red beard reputedly haunts one of the bedrooms here. He is thought to be one of the hanged smugglers. This spirit put in numerous performances in the 1950's, 60's and 70's but has not been as frequent of late. A landlord in the 70's decided that the haunting smuggler was one of his ancestors but the link was tenuous to say the least.

Before leaving The Royal Oak I feel bound to remark upon one of the present landlord's condolences to modernisation. A plaque in the gent's loo proudly states that this is the first Drain Doctor waterless urinal in Sussex. I wonder what the spiritual smuggler thinks of this. I should imagine he was a bucket and spade man.

SPREAD EAGLE HOTEL
MIDHURST

The Spread Eagle is part of the crest of Norman de Bohuns who settled his family at Cowdray Park. There was once a Spread Eagle just up the road at Fernhurst that seems to bear out this supposition.

The Earl of Southampton built Cowdray Park in 1530. Much of the building was destroyed by fire in 1793. Enough remains however to be an impressive ruin. Some of the building was almost untouched by the fire; outhouses and various estate buildings still exist, inflicting their horrendous yellow paintwork upon the unsuspecting eye.

The Spread Eagle far outdates its neighbour. It is reputed to have been built in 1430 with further extensions in1650. This is the epitome of the English inn. It so impressed Hilaire Belloc (Sussex's famous poet), that he described it as 'the oldest and most revered of all the prime inns of the world'.

It was certainly good enough for Elizabeth I to stay overnight and another monarch, Edward VII, also lodged here when he opened his nearby sanatorium. As well as Belloc, that writing genius H G Wells, a former pupil at the Grammar School, was a regular caller.

Little has changed in this most famous of old inns. Although a couple of extra buildings seem to have sprung up since my last visit, the black and white timbered old building is no less impressive. The attractive grounds still filter their way down to the ducks at the Old Mill Pond.

A recent visit assured me that The Spread Eagle Hotel still sported its oak beams, open fires and Hogarth's prints. I did not have time to ascertain if the Coal Hole Bar still has its full compliment of sore headed patrons, or if the old four poster is still upstairs inseparable from its famous wig cupboard.

What a rich and fertile ground for our spiritual friends one might think. It would be easy to imagine a spectre opening every other ancient doorway, exuding from every open fireplace or shinning along each ancient beam. Unfortunately ghosts at The Spread Eagle are sparse, timid and inept. Although stories abounded years ago there is very little other than the odd unexplained tapping to report. Rather disappointing.

THE LION
NYETIMBER, Near PAGHAM

The sign of the lion is one of the oldest in the country. It's popularity is not only restricted to inn signs. It has been represented on the shields and banners of fighting men for centuries. The lion is thought to have emanated from the royal arms where it first appeared in the reign of Edward III.

The lion appears on our pub signs in various hues. Most frequently in red (John of Gaunt) and also often in white (Edward IV). Golden lions, associated with the Flemish breweries, are less frequent and rarer still are blue lions (Prince of Denmark). Black lions are unusual in England but more popular over the Welsh border.

Nyetimber is a small attractive village that has all but been consumed by Bognor Regis. It is adjacent to Pagham Harbour with its tidal mud flats and it's distinctive wild life. The Harbour is now a nature reserve of some 1000 acres. Following the Nyetimber signs I was through the village and into Pagham before I realised it.

I asked two small boys the way to The Lion at Nyetimber.

"You've just been past it mate," they said. "Go back past The Lamb, then opposite The Bear, next to the burnt out eating house, turn right into Nyetimber Lane. The Lion's down there on the left."

How refreshing to find a ten year old boy giving directions by pubs. It gives me hope for the future.

The Lion inn and restaurant is thought to date back to 1407 but an earlier building on the site is believed to have been mentioned in the Domesday Book It was no doubt a smugglers pub, with its geographical location it would have been difficult to be anything else. Stories of smuggling abound, well-supported by a spy window that looks out on the Downs, the direction the revenue men would approach from Chichester.

Readers who have read any of my previous books on the subject will realise that I greet stories of underground tunnels with disdain and suspicion. Their convenience seldom justifies their expense. However the story that a subterranean passage connects The Lion with nearby Barton Manor is possible but indeed unlikely.

The Lion has seen many changes over the centuries; there is a Georgian front, an Elizabethan fireplace, a quaint winding staircase and a secret room behind the panels of an inglenook. The varying renovations and extensions over the years have resulted in the many different floor levels within the building. It is difficult to establish just how many secret rooms have been discovered over the years. Bedroom numbers have changed but I have been informed that there was once a blocked off door behind bedroom number 5, leading God knows where, and another in room 7 leading to the top of the house.

I arrived at The Lion at Christmas 1998. It was all that a British pub should be and more. Dining tables were set out for the expected host of Yuletide diners and the landlord and landlady were busy organising the many raffles and other festivities that abound at this time of year. I selected a malt whisky from the 200 that are kept in regular supply. The landlord is justly proud of this achievement. Row upon row of every conceivable brand is regimented in optics behind the bar. There is also a leaflet supplied naming each malt and the distillery from whence it came. I asked if I should be able to take a photograph of this splendid array and was greeted in the affirmative.

As may well be expected the haunting of The Lion is associated with smuggling. The girlfriend of a freebooter was seeing too much of a young revenue officer. It was thought that she might be talking a little too much and justice was swift and without appeal. She was done to death on the spot. We are not told how this young lady was hastened off this mortal coil nor whether or not her guilt was proven or presumed. This story is very similar to the one I covered at nearby Hayling Island in 'Haunted Inns of Hampshire'. Even to the extent that brandy and wine remains hidden under the floors. Both spectral ladies are witnessed assuming a position of searching.

The lady at The Lion is heard more often than seen, but when visibly witnessed she has unique capability in the spirit world of being able to change her attire. The spectral lady has been described as being 'tall, white faced and dressed in flowing black robes'. Another description, just days after, describes her as 'a tall lady in a white dress and bonnet'.

There are possibly two explanations for this discrepancy of attire. One is that the more scientific amongst ghost hunters suggest that they may sometimes appear as in an old fashioned photographic negative in which black and white are reversed. Or secondly, that The Lion has two female spirits, one wandering the upstairs bedrooms and the other down below searching for the entrance to the old tunnel; the subterranean passageway to Barton Manor, in which lay hidden 50 kegs of brandy and wine.

I did not question the busy staff but as I left I wished the landlady the 'compliments of the season'. She returned my good wishes.

"Have you seen anything of your resident ghost?" I asked.

"Oh yes," she replied in earnest, "She locked me out of my bedroom the other night."

Enough said.

THE ANGEL
PETWORTH

The old angel sign denoted the purity of all that lay beyond the door of the inn. The suggestion was that both host and wares were untainted and of the highest quality. In short the angel outside is guarding paradise within.

What has always foxed me is that signs of 'The Angel' always show a puritanical female with golden hair and wings, surely everybody knows that all worthwhile angels are of the male gender. Women are far too devious to attain absolute purity. Michael, Gabriel, Raphael and Urial to name but a few. Bet you can't name me four females.

Whilst on the subject of religious inn signs, and, at the risk of repeating myself from an early book; why is it that in every pub sign depicting Adam and Eve, Adam always has a navel? It seems a bit pointless to me. But I procrastinate.

I heard about The Angel at Petworth whilst staying in the Peak District. A discussion with a local unearthed this little gem. I had all but finished 'Haunted Inns of Sussex' but I decided on my return home to pop down to Petworth and have a look at it. Nobody goes to Petworth, everybody drives around it displaying their skills at the wheel and seeing how many battle scars they can obtain from the unforgiving walls of the town.

I had not walked around Petworth for a dozen years and if I catch the underhanded sneaky little berk who is turning good old pubs into antique shops, I shall personally place him amongst the angels. Petworth has followed such wonderfully pub abundant old towns as Hungerford in Berkshire and Odiham in Hampshire into complete obliteration. To add insult to injury some of the old names are retained, 'The Red Lion Antique Shop' etc.

I could see The Angel just up the hill from where I had parked, a beautiful old coaching inn. It was 10:45 a.m., knowing that most pubs in small rural towns open around 11 a.m. I sauntered down to examine the goods of my favourite antique shop, Help the Aged.

At 11:10 am I opened the door of The Angel. I was met by a congenial young man and his dog. He explained that The Angel was no longer an inn and did not serve alcohol. It was a private guesthouse and still did bed and breakfast.

'Beam me up Scottie, I can take no more!'

Before I did actually leave I did have a two-minute conversation with mine host. I do not approve of the direct approach but after an eighty-mile round trip I had no alternative.

"Is the old place still haunted?" I ventured.

"A lot of people have seen things here but personally I haven't. Good Morning."

Here is the story for what it is worth.

Many years ago an old maid servant 'lived in' at The Angel. She had been there so long that nobody could ever remember her abiding elsewhere. Over the years she had developed a firm friendship with another old lady in town. The two were inseparable and the old lady from town would often enjoy a drop of gin in the pubs inglenook whilst waiting for her friend from upstairs. One fateful day the old lady maid servant frightful of keeping her friend waiting rushed down the stairs, tripped on her long skirt and fell heavily, breaking her neck in the process. Her poor friend pined away and died of a broken heart. She refused ever to enter the inn again, in life that is, but she did enter it again in death. It is her spiritual form that is occasionally still witnessed by the inglenook, patiently awaiting her friend to come downstairs.

THE STAR
RUSPER

The most popular explanation of the star sign is that it has religious connotations. The Star represents the guiding light followed by the magi to an inn's stable, I'm sure you have heard the story.

An ancient and mysterious part of Sussex is this, not lessened by the close proximity of several major roads. There is a plethora of ancient manor houses in the area, their properties adorned by stables and duckponds.

Rusper has several attractive, half timbered and tile hung cottages. There are a couple of ancient inns and a post office. I am told that a Benedictine monastery once stood here but the last remnants of construction disappeared in 1781.

The church is still very much in evidence with its massive 16TH century tower.

The Star Inn is ancient indeed, both externally and internally. The building is reckoned to be 14TH century. Since then it has incorporated an adjacent cottage and also undergone the addition of an extension. The bar area is interesting, on one of the lower beams is written 'I drink to make others interesting!' On another, unfortunately, is the time weary inept 'Duck or Grouse'. There is a massive open fire and some tastefully done memorabilia on the walls.

I called in on The Star one overcast morning after dropping friends at Gatwick. A well-educated young man, obviously destined for better things, was torn between the dual duties of keeping the fire going and polishing the cutlery. I ordered a coffee to my shame and inspected the memorabilia. I studied a poem that was displayed in a dark corner and in microscopic print. "Surely nobody can read this without a magnifying glass," I ventured. "No," came the reply. "It was written years ago by a local poet. We used to have it on the back of our menus but people stole them."

I chatted for a while about the inn in general then inquired "Have you a resident ghost?"

"We certainly have, Sir. She is a lady who sits on the stool that you're on. We haven't seen her lately, I don't think she gets on with the new owners."

There was little else to be said. There has been some minor poltergeist activity here, if one accepts the turning on of light switches and beer taps. Personally I don't.

Incidentally, I believe I am the only ghost hunter to do a survey on ghost gender. When one disregards such phenomena as phantom objects, coaches, horses, dogs, fays, fairies and strange noises 85% of the remaining ghosts are female as opposed to 15% being of the male gender.

We already know that the average woman outlives us men by some 15-20 years. Is life so pleasant for women that they find it necessary to hang around the other side of the curtain?

THE CRAB AND LOBSTER
SIDLESHAM, Near PAGHAM, WEST SUSSEX

This sign is typical of many which are found in numerous ports. It advertises the local produce of which the populace is justly proud.

Sidlesham now sprawls along the Chichester to Selsey road. It is an extremely long village, which appears to have no centre. The actual centre is way off of the main road at the head of a creek, just north of Pagham Harbour. Sidlesham was a bustling port until late in the 19TH century. The Crab and Lobster was reputedly used by Nelson's crew as they came ashore to collect grain. For varying reasons, predominately silting, Sidlesham became a backwater, a very attractive backwater and these days a very expensive backwater.
The history of The Crab and Lobster is very much the history of Sidlesham.
Anybody who has read anything of the English Civil War will realise just how complicated matters were. Neighbouring towns just a few miles apart were occupied by opposing factions. If one were to make even the broadest generalisation, it would be that in the latter stages, parliamentary troops seemed to hold many towns whilst the rural areas seemed to sympathise with the King. In West Sussex confusion reigned with troops marching and counter marching in all directions. Such towns as Horsham and Chichester remained royalist but their defences were withering. Finally Chichester stood alone but firmly under siege. It was than that the port of Sidlesham became its only lifeline. The ancient inn that once stood where The Crab and Lobster now stands was the safe house of fleeing royalists.
When Chichester fell to Cromwell's forces, isolated royalists made for the old inn. One such man was a prosperous local landowner named Sir Robert Earnley. Gathering two close friends and two nephews he made a successful attempt to reach Sidlesham. Unfortunately for Sir Robert and company they were surprised by a patrol of parliamentary troopers. After a swift running skirmish all five royalists lay dead or dying. Sir Robert Earnley was carried into the inn to expire.
It will not take the more astute reader long before he hazards a guess as to who reputedly haunts The Crab and Lobster. For many years there have been reports of a gentleman in cavalier costume briefly appearing both inside and outside The Crab and Lobster. In the 60's the then time landlord's experiences became a lot less vague. His cats

gave parts of the floor a very wide berth, heavy footsteps were heard but the owner never traced and a room upstairs was virtually abandoned because of its inexplicable evil atmosphere. Also a prowler was heard downstairs, but when the landlord arrived suitably armed with a shotgun he found no one and everything locked and bolted.

Possibly the strangest little episode at The Crab and Lobster occurred in 1969. A lady who had dined there was talking to the landlord. As they chatted socially she glanced into the saloon bar, the lady turned white, stood transfixed and pointed into the room. When she had regained her composure the lady related that she had seen a dying cavalier trying desperately to staunch the flow of blood from a wound with a handkerchief.

The story goes that when the lady had left, the landlord's wife noticed the name in which the table had been booked was that of a famous medium.

Why am I always deeply suspicious of mediums? The lady may have heard the well-known story of the dying cavalier and taken the opportunity to enhance her reputation. I personally heard that story many years ago from a local, a proper local that is, not one of the rootless affluent outsiders who have purchased so much hereabouts.

Straight faced I listened to every detail of the slayings and hauntings. However, I had to contain a wry smile when the local related earnestly that Sir Robert's soul had escaped through his mouth and was still trapped in the attic.

Little had changed when I looked into The Crab and Lobster for a drink one Sunday lunchtime. There is a definite atmosphere hereabouts but I believe it to be more akin to Pagham Harbour and the road outside rather than the inn itself. However, I could not help myself taking the occasional glance into the saloon just in case there was the odd cavalier lying around.

THE WHITE HORSE
STORRINGTON, WEST SUSSEX

The White Horse is one of the country's five most popular signs. It celebrates a local equine hero or heroine. The exalted horse pictured on the sign could have been a local hunter, a leader of some coach team or just a plodding parochial character.

Storrington is an attractive village some ten miles north of Worthing. It is fine hilly country with captivating viewpoints. Nearby Kithurst Hill (700 feet) with its preserved Celtic fields is a fine example. Sullington Warren is a pleasant National Trust property in the area. Elizabethan Parham, which dates from 1577, is worth a visit for it's long gallery and near Manor Farm there is a massive tithe barn dating from 1685.

The White Horse dates from 1535, two years after the birth of Elizabeth I. Incidentally it was in this year that Sir Thomas More was executed. In later days Sir Arnold Bax, the composer, was an almost permanent guest. There is a smart and impressive commemorative plaque upon the wall.

Today the front exterior is a little flat and uninteresting. It has obviously been extended. I arrived on a Saturday morning. I was a little concerned by a large sign on the door advertising Sky TV, but once inside, The White Horse is impressive. It is large, clean, homely and friendly a true locals pub.

There are two large bars, a restaurant and apparently a number of bedrooms. I could not help overhearing a politically correct barman explaining to a punter that an attractively challenged lady had been looking for him the previous night. I thought this to be a fine example of the camaraderie of the place.

There would seem to be a number of ghosts at The White Horse. Several landlords over the years have experienced the 'Phantom Nudger'. A nudger is not an unusual type of physic phenomenon, it is an invisible sort of spectre that gives its victim a sharp push or nudge. The White Horse's nudger however went a little further than most, by actually picking an ex-landlady off of her feet.

As with most physic phenomena, the mild poltergeist activity is proceeded by, or accompanied by, a sharp fall in temperature. Footsteps have been heard and a strange feeling of depression prevails.

For a short postscript to The White Horse, I am indebted to Guy Playfair a ghost hunter of fame and tenacity.

The aforementioned Sir Arnold Bex, the honoured guest, had been dead a quarter of a century when a letter turned up at The White Horse addressed to his executors. It was Christmas time so the landlady locked the letter in the composer's old room until after the holiday. When retrieving the letter to return it to the post office, a discernible smudge was seen upon the envelope, almost as if it had been trodden on.

Make of that what you will.

HALF MOON
WARNINGLID

A stranger sign than it might first appear. There are hundreds of 'Suns' about the country but very few 'Moons'; full, half, crescent or otherwise.

There is very little in heraldry concerning moons. There was one on the coat of arms of the Monson family of Lincolnshire, however that would not explain the sign in other parts of the country. We have a Sun and Moon in London which is probably the combination of two separate pubs and a Moon and Sixpence in Wales, which is probably named after a famous short story. Let us assume that most 'Moons' were painted on signs as 'Half Moons' and the sign suggested the name instead of the more usual vice-versa.

Warninglid, is a stones throw from the M23 and about fifteen minutes from Gatwick, it possesses a school and a pub but no shop. Take it from one who did a seven-mile round trip for a packet of cigars.

The Half Moon is a 15TH century building constructed of Sussex stone. It has half-panelled walls, open log fires and horse brasses. It did not become a pub until 1850, so the Irish landlord told me. He also told me that 18 pilots lived in the village and that he was having trouble with a small minded local council that would not let him extend.

The ghostly experiences at the Half Moon are tenuous and infrequent. I had heard the audible squealings and scratchings had been experienced but nothing had ever manifested into anything visual.

What is strange is that in a second conversation with the landlord I asked what the building was before its reincarnation as a pub. It was obviously too small for a private house.

"It was a farm cottage," he said.

"Surely it was too small," I replied.

"No," he said. "Some of the outbuildings have been included. Where you are standing was a slaughterhouse."

This instantly made me wonder about the reported squealing and scratching.

"Have you got a ghost?" I ventured.

"Depends," he replied.

"Depends on what?" I returned.

"Depends if you are American or not."

I assured my host that I was born and bred in the Royal County of Berkshire.

"No point then," came the wonderful Irish brogue reply. "I'll save my repertoire for the Yanks, they'll believe anything."

I did not pursue my enquiries.

Any ghost hunter should leave Warninglid well-alone. Ancient as it may be, the presence of eighteen technically efficient airline pilots would dissuade any self-respecting ghost from approaching.